Inclusion Coaching FOR Collaborative Schools

Inclusion Coaching for Collaborative Schools

Toby J. Karten

CORWIN
A SAGE Company

CORWIN
A SAGE Company

FOR INFORMATION:

Corwin

A SAGE Company

2455 Teller Road

Thousand Oaks, California 91320

(800) 233-9936

www.corwin.com

SAGE Publications Ltd.

1 Oliver's Yard

55 City Road

London EC1Y 1SP

United Kingdom

SAGE Publications India Pvt. Ltd.

B 1/I 1 Mohan Cooperative Industrial Area

Mathura Road, New Delhi 110 044

India

SAGE Publications Asia-Pacific Pte. Ltd.

3 Church Street

#10-04 Samsung Hub

Singapore 049483

Acquisitions Editor: Jessica Allan

Associate Editor: Julie Nemer

Editorial Assistant: Heidi Arndt

Production Editors: Cassandra Margaret Seibel
and Melanie Birdsall

Copy Editor: Melinda Masson

Typesetter: C&M Digitals (P) Ltd.

Proofreader: Caryne Brown

Indexer: Wendy Allex

Cover Designer: Gail Buschman

Permissions Editor: Karen Ehrmann

Printed in the United States of America

Library of Congress Cataloging-in-Publication Data

A catalog record of this book is available from the Library of Congress.

ISBN: 978-1-4522-6821-7

This book is printed on acid-free paper.

SUSTAINABLE FORESTRY INITIATIVE
Certified Chain of Custody
Promoting Sustainable Forestry
www.sfiprogram.org
SFI-01268
SFI label applies to text stock

13 14 15 16 17 10 9 8 7 6 5 4 3 2 1

Contents

PART III: STRENGTHS AND CHALLENGES OF INCLUSION

PART IV: PROFESSIONAL DEVELOPMENT

PART V: INCLUSION COACHING REALITIES

Acknowledgments

Thanks to all of the dedicated professionals, families, and students who continually, seamlessly, patiently, and collaboratively discover ways to make inclusion work. Learners with disabilities who are included in the general education classroom shine when everyone believes that successful outcomes are the bottom line. Inclusion then goes beyond the legislative mandates since the general education classroom becomes not only the first option of service, but also the best one possible for students with and without disabilities. Kudos to all of you!

Additional thanks go to the following people at Corwin who are my collaborative partners and coaches. Jessica Allan, my acquisitions editor, your sage advice and guidance are greatly appreciated and respected. Thanks to associate editor Julie Nemer, editorial assistant Lisa Whitney, production editors Cassandra Margaret Seibel and Melanie Birdsall, cover designer Gail Buschman, and copy editor Melinda Masson. Your assistance at each step of the book's production is immeasurable and defines how Corwin facilitates an environment of high expectations and professionalism.

Finally, I'd like to include thanks to my husband, son, family, colleagues, and friends who offer their ongoing support. The world is a fun place with you by my side. Let's continue to collaborate.

PUBLISHER'S ACKNOWLEDGMENTS

Corwin gratefully acknowledges the contributions of the following reviewers:

Andrea Hume, NBCT
Special Education Teacher
Oakdale Elementary School
Dedham, MA

Kelli S. Kercher
Special Education Team Leader
Murray City School District
Murray, UT

Karen Kozy-Landress
Speech/Language Pathologist
MILA Elementary School
Merritt Island, FL

Carol Spencer
Director of Curriculum
Addison Northwest Supervisory Union
Vergennes, VT

About the Author

 **Toby J. Karten** is an experienced educator who has been immersed in the field of special education for her entire career. As an accomplished author and researcher, she has presented successful staff development to local, national, and international audiences. Toby is a lecturer at Drew and Monmouth Universities and an adjunct professor and graduate instructor at the Regional Training Center, which is affiliated with Gratz College, College of New Jersey, and Washington College. Being involved in the field of special education for the past three decades has afforded Ms. Karten an opportunity to help many children and adults from elementary through graduate levels around the world. She has been a resource teacher, a staff developer, an adult educator, and an inclusion coach and consultant in New York and New Jersey schools and in many districts nationally and globally. In addition to assuming roles as inclusion coach, student and family advocate, professional developer, mentor, and resource teacher, Toby designed a graduate course titled *Skills and Strategies for Inclusion and disABILITY Awareness* and has trained other instructors in three states to teach her course. She has been recognized by both the Council for Exceptional Children and the New Jersey Department of Education as an exemplary educator, receiving two Teacher of the Year awards. She earned an undergraduate degree in special education from Brooklyn College, a master of science in special education from the College of Staten Island, a supervisory degree from Georgian Court University, and an honorary doctorate from Gratz College. Toby has authored several books and resources about inclusion practices, which are currently used for instruction on many college and university campuses and in schools throughout the world.

Ms. Karten is married and has a son and a few dogs. She enjoys teaching, reading, writing, artwork, and, most of all, learning. As the author of this book, she believes that inclusion does not begin and end in the classroom, but is a philosophy that continues throughout life. Hence, inclusion is not only research-based but life-based as well!

Introduction

The teaching profession today involves both students and educators being consummate learners. Research offers opportunities, but instructional coaches assist with the implementation. The role of an inclusion coach is a collaborative one that is intended to help school leaders view inclusion through a positive lens to build teams of players who are prepared to face inclusion challenges with effective strategies across the curriculum. Schools in the United States—from Florida to Seattle to New York City—as well as in Canada, have inclusion coaches who are formally given that name, while other schools have a variety of people who assume that role—for example, learning disabilities teacher consultants, supervisors, instructional coaches, and principals. It may be a new position in some schools or delegated to experienced special or general education personnel or team leaders, mentors, or coaches who are already on staff, in addition to outside educational consultants who help move the inclusion needle. Schools that do not have inclusion coaches are now realizing the importance of offering teachers this type of collaborative, structured, and ongoing support to promote both student and educator success.

This resource promotes inclusion as a viable and beneficial setting for students when it matches and correlates the needs of individual students, educators, and classrooms with appropriate instruction and supports. *Inclusion,* a term that is not defined in educational legislation, occurs each day in neighborhood schools when students with and without disabilities learn side by side with their age-level peers in the general education classroom. *Coaching* offers professional and respectful support and feedback within trusting pedagogical relationships. *Collaboration* occurs when ideas and resources are shared and reflected upon to formulate new plans, improve current ones, and move forward in programs. And last, but not least, a *school* is a place where students are taught knowledge and skills alongside their peers. Thereby—as its title, *Inclusion Coaching for Collaborative Schools,* indicates—this resource offers professional ways for educational communities to collectively apply these terms to benefit learners of all ability levels with care and concern for the students and educators as well as the concept of inclusion.

Inclusive school environments are the preparatory settings that allow individuals with disabilities to be part of inclusive societies. The legislation states that students are to receive a free and appropriate public education in the least restrictive environment. Students today are often offered an education within the general education classroom accompanied by the supplementary supports and services. How this inclusive education occurs requires systematic thought, preparation, and ongoing professionalism. Administrators, teacher leaders, supervisors, coaches, general and special educators, families, and students are aware that inclusion is a complex process. Students with disabilities comprise a heterogeneous group. This range includes students with significant intellectual disabilities along with students with diverse emotional, behavioral, social, language, sensory, communicative, motor, and learning needs. The physical placement of students with disabilities in the general education class from preschool onward begins the inclusive process, but providing the necessary and ongoing resources, supports, and services to both students and educators ensures that students' academic, social, emotional, behavioral, and communicative goals are achieved.

Ideal inclusive settings do not exist without much labor and preparation. Administrators, educators, related staff, students, and their families collaboratively formulate and shape the inclusive factors. There are benefits derived when school leaders offer educators collaborative opportunities. This includes higher teacher satisfaction and student achievement (Guarino, Santibanez, & Daley, 2006; Kardos & Johnson, 2007). Veteran teachers share responsibilities with newer teachers, and professional growth is increased for all with curriculum, instruction, and professional development (Goddard, Goddard, & Taschannen-Moran, 2007). This collaboration ranges from having more planning time together, to observing one another, to classroom management, to mapping lesson units of study, to inclusion strategies, and more. Together, all parties ensure that the inclusive environment is an appropriate one for students with and without disabilities. Inclusion coaching practices allow learners to thrive from being placed in the inclusion setting, instead of students facing frustrations or educators becoming overwhelmed. Inclusion requires that each school and classroom effectively include students with the appropriate lessons, supports, and strategies. This resource propagates that inclusion coaching within a collaborative environment helps everyone to continually implement and reflect on the best inclusion choices for school structures and classroom practices.

Inclusion, although never a generic program, has basic governing rules. The following five two-word sentences sound simplistic, but as the book unfolds, each of these inclusion rules will be expanded on to be certain that *inclusion* always *rules!* These pictorial symbols appear on corresponding pages when they come into play, the goal being for these icons to be internalized into each and every inclusive setting.

Basic Inclusion Rules:

1. Be professional.

2. Be compassionate.

3. Be structured.

4. Be aware.

5. Be reflective.

Overall, rules help us move forward and boost productivity, yet each inclusion classroom and grade has different students, teachers, and curriculum standards that require individual considerations and appropriate inclusion applications. Countries around the world, along with private and public organizations, *including schools,* are governed and influenced by rules. Rules are tweaked over time; hence the U.S. Constitution was written, followed by the Bill of Rights with amendments to accommodate different situations. School districts have local education agencies, parent committees, boards of education, administrative directives, and instructional student support teams that discuss, debate, enforce, and amend district policies and practices. Individualized education programs (IEPs) are written and then reviewed; inclusion rules and coaching strategies also require ongoing review.

Good leadership guides its staff with clear signals, consistent focus, and appropriate actions that are directed toward improvements (McClure, 2008). This book affirms that inclusion coaches are a collaborative part of this process to help teachers and students achieve high results.

This resource is sectioned into five parts. Part I of *Inclusion Coaching for Collaborative Schools* offers a foundation of collaborative inclusion knowledge and defines the coaching roles of administrators, learning support teams, educators, teacher mentors, co-teachers, related staff, families, and students. It includes information about learners and descriptive ways that school decision makers, coaches, and educators ensure that inclusion is embraced and implemented within appropriate school and classroom structures. Part II establishes coaching baselines and offers ideas on how the inclusion principles are aligned to learner profiles with lesson differentiation, inclusion goals, norms, planning, strategies, and curriculum practices that align with the Common Core State Standards. A consideration for the needs of whole classes, small groups, and individual students and for the importance of reviewing results is delineated. English language arts, math, and cross-disciplinary lessons are connected to the inclusion principles and coaching rules. Part III talks about the strengths and challenges of inclusion with factors such as scheduling, funding, co-teaching responsibilities, how to close the gaps and ambiguities, and addressing the attitudes that appear within shared environments and individual classrooms. Coaching planners and staff activities are offered. Part IV outlines ideas for specific professional development actions, ranging from learning more about disabilities to formulating professional roles with inclusion bridges that maximize individual competencies. This includes outlining 21st century inclusion competencies from teams to peers and book clubs. Part V invites readers to have inclusion inferences beyond the data to think about the longevity of inclusion in their environments to ensure ongoing student achievements. Inclusion coaching vignettes and curriculum connections are offered. Delineated activities threaded throughout the book also offer ways to engage staff in reflective and collaborative inclusion practices. As denoted by icon in the margin, many of these forms are also available online as downloadable PDFs. Inclusion coaching strategies require professional collaboration, structure, compassion, awareness, and reflections that connect the learning to each and every student and educator. The first chapter begins with the most important people involved, namely, the students. Refer to Table I.1 for an overview, and then read on for more specifics.

Table I.1 Inclusion Coaching for Collaborative Schools at a Glance

	Activities and Documents	*Objectives for School Leaders*
Part I *Collaborative Inclusion Knowledge*	Figure 1.1 Sample Individualized Education Program Form	To offer a model of essential elements to include in students' individualized education programs
	Figure 2.1 Inclusion Coaching Checklist	To plot staff baseline levels of communication, leadership, and professionalism for inclusion improvement plans
	Figure 2.2 Inclusion Coaching Notes: Sample Lesson Figure 2.3 Inclusion Coaching Notes: Template	To present a template to organize and share thoughts with educators during coaching debriefing sessions
	Figure 2.4 Response to Intervention (RTI) Form	To provide structure for staff to review whole-class, small-group, and individual student responses to intervention at set time periods each marking period
	Figure 2.5 Benefits and Challenges of Co-Teaching Models Figure 2.6 Positive Co-Teaching Actions Figure 2.7 Reflecting on Our Co-Teaching Practices	To invite educators to vary their co-teaching models
	Figure 2.8 Family Collaborations: Proactive Approaches	To develop healthy homeschool partnerships by collaboratively formulating an agreed-upon set of responsibilities for each environment
	Figure 2.9 Communication Logs	To encourage staff to continually document family contacts
	Figure 3.1 INCLUDE Planner	To plan annual, monthly, and weekly inclusion actions to individualize, naturalize, collaborate, communicate, learn, understand, and evaluate
Part II *Establishing Inclusion Coaching Baselines*	Inclusion Coaching Agenda	To offer a model timeline of annual inclusion topics for general and special education teachers
	Figure 4.1 Inclusion Principle 7: Applicable Standards-Based Curriculum Example Figure 4.2 Inclusion Principle 5: Applicable Standards-Based Curriculum Example Figure 4.3 Inclusion Principle 14: Applicable Standards-Based Curriculum Example	To highlight basic inclusion principles for coaches and educators
	Figure 4.4 Inclusion Principle 17: Applicable Standards-Based Curriculum Example	To remind educators to think of ways to increase student self-awareness of levels and progress

Part II	Figure 4.5 How I/We Will Infuse These Big Ideas into Lessons	To invite educators to apply 18 principles to learners across populations, subjects, and grade levels
	Figure 4.6 Inclusion Norms: Establishment and Expectations	To collaboratively establish inclusion norms and expectations at the beginning of each school year
Establishing Inclusion Coaching Baselines	Figure 4.7 Big Ideas of Inclusion	To help educators focus on the objectives, procedures, assessments, and follow-ups of inclusion classroom coaching programs
	Figure 5.1 Class Monitoring and Curriculum-Based Assessments and Weekly Interventions	To offer a sample of types of accommodations and modifications for both instruction and assessments
	Figure 5.2 Inclusion Survey	To obtain feedback from staff before coaching sessions begin to determine current inclusion and co-teaching levels, experiences, and concerns and to structure the coaching and professional development
	Figure 5.3 Learner Profile: Example Figure 5.4 Learner Profile: Professional Activity	To collaboratively highlight and match students' strengths and interests with social, emotional, behavioral, physical, and communicative objectives
	Figure 5.5a Differentiation Rubric	To offer staff the categories and degrees of lesson differentiation
	Figure 5.5b Differentiation Ideas	To allow educators an opportunity to plan a differentiated unit of study
	Figure 6.1 Curriculum Goals at a Glance Figure 6.2 Quarterly Lesson Plan Units for Reading and Language Arts (Second Grade) Figure 6.3 Algebra II Figure 6.4 Physics Class Quarterly Plans Figure 6.5 Quarterly Lesson Plan Units	To encourage staff to outline unit objectives for each quarter and month at the onset of the year
	Figure 6.6 Applying the CCSS for English Language Arts to Inclusive Classrooms	To offer a model for staff to see how English language arts standards-based lesson objectives are delivered to the whole class, small groups, and individual students
	Figure 6.7 Eight CCSS Standards of Mathematical Practice: Grades K–12	To apply Common Core State Standards math practices to classroom scenarios to increase student achievement
	Figure 6.8 Let's Do This Together: Cross-Curricular Planner to Strengthen Connections	To invite educators to share their plans with each other to tap into one another's strengths, insights, and collaborative expertise to develop cross-curricular lessons

(Continued)

Table I.1   (Continued)

Part III	Figure 8.1 Inclusion Structures for Educators and Students	To offer inclusion practices and nonexamples
Strengths and Challenges of Inclusion	Figure 8.2 Inclusion Coaching: Our Goals for the Year	To present a sample August–June agenda of annual goals for a K–6 school
	Figure 8.3 Communications Between an Inclusion Coach and K–6 Teachers	To delineate co-teacher concerns, plans, goals, and strategies to strengthen partnerships
	Figure 8.4 Middle School Team Meetings	To review the communications of educators of students in Grades 5–8 with corresponding action plans and coaching recommendations
	Figure 8.5 Inclusion Coaching Planning Sheet: My/Our Thoughts About . . .	To invite educators to express their inclusion thoughts about differentiated lessons, applying appropriate strategies and classroom structures
	Figure 9.1 Disability-Curriculum Analogies	To generate discussion and promote positive attitudes about disabilities
	Inclusion and Co-Teaching Wish List	To discuss effective co-teaching structures
	Assessment Insights	To increase professional knowledge of assessments and resources
Part IV	Figure 11.1 Inclusion Frameworks	To increase collaborative knowledge of inclusion practices that consider the planning, preparation, environments, instructional strategies, and professional development
	Figure 11.2 Our Inclusion Framework	To encourage professionals to prepare, create, collaborate, communicate, and learn more about successful inclusion factors
Professional Development	Figure 11.3 Council for Exceptional Children: Initial-Level Special Education Preparation Standards (Beginning Special Education Professionals) Figure 11.4 CEC Special Education Specialist Advanced Preparation Standards	To increase staff knowledge of professional standards and associated skills
	Figure 11.5 Online Resources and Professional Organizations	To encourage professional exploration of available inclusion resources
	Figure 11.6 Learning More About Student Populations Within an Inclusive Classroom Figure 11.7 Collaboration: An Essential, Continual Step	To offer online investigation of different disabilities students present within general education classrooms to promote collaborative next steps
	Journal and Magazine Choices	To offer staff journals and magazines as resources to capitalize on the knowledge to advance professional growth and, in turn, students' skills

Part IV *Professional Development*	Figure 12.1a Team Planner	To invite staff to continually document inclusion interventions at scheduled planning dates
	Figure 12.1b Formative and Summative Progress Monitoring and Assessment Notes	To encourage professionals to keep quarterly anecdotal notes on students
	Figure 12.2 Books to Gain Increased Sensitivities and Knowledge About disABILITIES	To provide titles of adult reads about disABILITIES across genres for professional book clubs to discuss and learn more about differences
	Literature Ties: *The Don't-Give-Up Kid and Learning Differences* *The Man Who Loved Clowns* *Singing Hands*	To offer bibliotherapy choices on elementary and secondary levels to increase students' knowledge of disabilities
Part V *Inclusion Coaching Realities*	Figure 14.1 Inclusion Curriculum Coaching Connections	To relate inclusion coaching to curriculum examples
	Figure 14.2 Sixth-Grade Social Studies Assignment: Original and Compartmentalized	To offer snapshots of inclusion coaching scenarios and curriculum connections
	Figure 15.1 Revisiting Inclusion Rules	To encourage staff to reflect on how they plan to continually apply structure, awareness, compassion, professional collaboration, and reflection in inclusive classrooms
	Figure 15.2 Inclusion Coaching Is as Easy as the ABCs	To remind professionals of all of the collaborative inclusion coaching basics

PART I

Collaborative Inclusion Knowledge

1

The Students

Although some of this beginning material is basic knowledge, many schools do not ascertain whether or not educators have the necessary foundational information about the appropriate characteristics and strategies for learners with disabilities and the legislative requirements. Students in inclusion classrooms present varying learning, social, behavioral, emotional, communicative, physical, perceptual, sensory, and cultural levels, backgrounds, and challenges that require specific instructional plans and strategies (Boscardin, Mainzer, & Kealy, 2011; Karten, 2010b, 2010c). This diversity necessitates the thoughtful and innovative expertise of leaders and coaches who collaboratively assist general and special educators to help students achieve their highest potentials while enforcing and honoring each student's and family's legislative rights.

Principals, curriculum supervisors, school leaders, teacher leaders, and school intervention coaches assume the role of an inclusion coach to ensure that students receive the appropriate education, while some districts also hire the professional direction of outside inclusion coaches. Collective voices determine and apply the appropriate strategies and student interventions. No one possesses a monopoly on the strategies since a team approach values diverse experiences and perspectives. The ongoing collaborative and inclusive insights connect to a spectrum of learners, families, and educators with pedagogical structure that positively impacts students with and without disabilities to achieve successful postsecondary outcomes. Peers and families must also be strong strategic partners, who look beyond a child's labeled disability to recognize his or her strengths. All parties therefore ensure that the highest level of learning is honored and achieved within a student's least restrictive environment (LRE).

Although there is diversity within each group of learners, the commonalities offered generate appropriate knowledge, skills, and strategies that principals, inclusion team leaders, and coaches share with their staff. Examples are delineated in the lists that follow for students with emotional, learning, and intellectual differences. The goal is for educators to expand on these lists with additional strategies and interventions for all populations of learners.

Students With an Emotional Difference

1. These students may display externalizing or internalizing behavior ranging from acting out to displaying defiance, to compulsivity, to being withdrawn or depressed.

2. In order to create a behavioral intervention plan (BIP) for students, conduct a functional behavioral assessment (FBA) that determines the reasons or triggers for the behavior (e.g., work is too hard or easy, student wants extra attention—be it negative or positive).

3. Although the characteristics of students with emotional and behavioral disorder (EBD) are not always as visible as other disabilities, they are real and cannot be dismissed as willful (e.g., just as a child who is blind or has a physical disability would not be asked to *see* or *walk* the right way, neither should a student with an emotional and behavioral disturbance be expected to *just behave*).

4. Proactive measures need to be in place, rather than having a *wait and see* attitude, with all staff receiving the knowledge and training with *what if* scenarios that delineate the nature of the behavior and what might be expected.

5. Enlist the expertise of school psychologists, counselors, social workers, and behavioral interventionists to formulate plans.

6. Offer structured and fair rules that are positive, observable, and measurable with associated consequences delineated and consistently enforced.

7. Examine polices and procedures to decide on appropriate scaffolding and accommodations that ensure the physical and emotional safety of all students.

8. Get to know students to connect with their interests and to offer the appropriate motivators for reinforcement schedules.

9. Offer realistic and timely feedback.

10. Educate peers about emotional differences and how they should react to behaviors.

Students With a Learning Difference

1. This group of learners displays intense diversity with a wide range of strengths and weaknesses. Attention, memory, and reasoning, as well as auditory and visual processing, may be impacted.

2. One-third of all students who receive special education (SE) services have a learning disability (U.S. Department of Education, 2010).

3. Types of learning disabilities include, but are not limited to, the following:

   a. *Dyslexia*—difficulties with reading, ranging from fluency to verbal expressions to knowing sounds of letters and/or comprehension of words and ideas

   b. *Dysgraphia*—difficulties with writing, ranging from physically forming letters to organizing thoughts in written expressions

   c. *Dyscalculia*—difficulties with mathematics, including counting, telling time, knowing number facts, computations, and problem solving

   d. *Dyspraxia*—difficulties with motor skills ranging from fine motor skills such as cutting or holding a pencil to large motor skills involving coordination in sports, general clumsiness, speech, and personal grooming

   e. *Dysphasia*—difficulties attaching meaning to language, including verbal skills, grammar, semantics, reading comprehension, information processing, and nonverbal messages

4. An overlapping of characteristics may often be presented under the label of another disability with students under these labels also having learning disabilities (LD) that are manifested within the inclusive classroom setting (e.g., attention deficit/hyperactivity disorder [ADHD], Asperger's, Tourette's, autism, auditory-processing disorders, receptive or expressive speech-language disorders).

5. There is no cure for a learning disability, but students learn to compensate for weaker areas with specific strategies that allow them to highlight and maximize their strengths (e.g., using graphic organizers to help with written expressions, mnemonics to assist with memory weaknesses, step-by-step approaches to learn more difficult mathematical procedures to solve word problems, multisensory approaches to learn to decode words, using a digital recorder to take notes, having spell-check to correct errors, using other accessible instructional materials ranging from text-to-speech tools to read and process written language to an AutoSummarize tool to highlight the key points in a longer reference page accessed online).

6. As per IDEA (the Individuals with Disabilities Education Act), students with learning disabilities do not include those with learning problems that are primarily the result of visual, hearing, or motor disabilities, of intellectual disability, of emotional disturbance, or of environmental, cultural, or economic disadvantage.

7. Local educational agencies do not exclusively look at a discrepancy between intellectual ability and achievement to determine an LD diagnosis, but are also permitted and encouraged to keep track of student performances in response to research-based interventions and alternative procedures before an individualized education program (IEP) is generated, which is part of response to intervention (RTI).

8. Appropriate accommodations and modifications are applicable for both instruction and assessments and are usually IEP driven, but never constant, since the idea is to promote learning, not learned helplessness.

9. All staff needs to be privy to the strategies that best help students (e.g., paraprofessionals, bus drivers, lunchroom aides, co-teachers, art, physical education, music teachers, and more).

10. Create self-regulated learners from the early grades and onward who are aware of their current levels and the necessary supports needed to increase their skills.

Students With an Intellectual Disability

1. Students learn, but in different ways (e.g., concrete presentations, step-by-step approaches that offer opportunities for additional repetition and practice, modeling, more opportunities for success).

2. More assistance with different approaches is required with social interactions, communications, self-help, and adaptive daily living skills (e.g., using iPads to interact with others, convey needs, or communicate responses).

3. Investigate critical early interventions (National Dissemination Center for Children with Disabilities, 2012).

4. Different levels of support are related to the degree of intellectual disability, or ID (e.g., self-contained vs. inclusive classroom).

5. As with other disabilities, students with intellectual disabilities need access to the general education (GE) curriculum with progress monitored and appropriate supports in place within inclusive environments, if that is determined to be the LRE.

6. Establish transitional plans that address academic and functional achievements (National Dissemination Center for Children with Disabilities, 2010).

7. Discover and connect to students' strengths, interests, and abilities.

8. Monitor progress toward reaching IEP goals.

9. Provide a structured peer-support system within the class and school with age-level peers who help students with ID to sharpen academic, social, and communicative skills.

10. Offer feedback on student progress strategies by establishing ongoing home communications.

Educators need to be aware of the basic disability legislation to provide appropriate services. According to federal legislation, specifically IDEA, the general education classroom is considered to be the first option of placement as the LRE for students who have a disability that affects their educational performance. An evaluation determines if a disability is present and, if so, the placement recommended. If the LRE is determined to be the general education classroom, then appropriate supplementary aids and related services each child needs must be present. IDEA provides services and protections for approximately 6.6 million students in the United States, which is about 13% of total student enrollment. Infants and toddlers under 3 years of age who experience developmental delays in cognitive, physical, communication, social or emotional, and adaptive development or have a diagnosed physical or mental condition that has a high probability of resulting in a developmental delay are also eligible for early intervention services. The 13 IDEA categories include the following ones for children aged 3 through 21. They can be better remembered by teachers with this 13-word acronymic sentence: *All very determined students deserve infinitely more opportunities than schools have ever offered.*

A utism

V isual impairment (including blindness)

D eafness

S pecific learning disability

D eafness-blindness

I ntellectual disability

M ultiple disabilities

O ther health impairment

T raumatic brain injury

S peech and language impairment

H earing impairment

E motional disturbance

O rthopedic impairment

An inclusive classroom is an appropriate setting for a student with a disability if the general education classroom, with the necessary supports and related services, is determined to meet that child's needs. It is often stated that special education is a service, not a place. Even though students may be eligible to receive services under an IDEA classification such as one of the 13 listed, it does not mean that stagnation is ever an option. There also need to be plans to think about reducing services, once students gain skills and can perform tasks and skills independently. Scaffolding is important, but so is fading out services if they are no longer appropriate ones. If students learn to be overly dependent, then that learned helplessness becomes an obstacle to future achievements as an independent and productive adult. If the obverse is true and services need to be increased, then that would be appropriate as well. Decisions should be based not on politics, preferences, or traditions, but on each student's diverse and individualized needs.

Although each state and district within that state may choose to vary the required IEP layout, Figure 1.1 offers a sample IEP form from the U.S. Department of Education's Office of Special Education and Rehabilitative Services (OSERS) that contains the essential IEP elements considered by educators and families as they formulate a student's IEP together.

Figure 1.1 Sample Individualized Education Program Form

Individualized Education Program

The Individualized Education Program (IEP) is a written document that is developed for each eligible child with a disability. The Part B regulations specify, at 34 CFR §§300.320–300.328, the procedures that school districts must follow to develop, review, and revise the IEP for each child. The document below sets out the IEP content that those regulations require.

A statement of the child's present levels of academic achievement and functional performance, including:

- How the child's disability affects the child's involvement and progress in the general education curriculum (i.e., the same curriculum as for nondisabled children) or <u>for preschool children</u>, as appropriate, how the disability affects the child's participation in appropriate activities. [34 CFR §300.320(a)(1)]

A statement of measurable annual goals, including academic and functional goals designed to:

- Meet the child's needs that result from the child's disability to enable the child to be involved in and make progress in the general education curriculum. [34 CFR §300.320(a)(2)(i)(A)]

- Meet each of the child's other educational needs that result from the child's disability. [34 CFR §300.320(a)(2)(i)(B)]

For children with disabilities who take alternate assessments aligned to alternate achievement standards (in addition to the annual goals), a description of benchmarks or short-term objectives. [34 CFR §300.320(a)(2)(ii)]

A description of:

- How the child's progress toward meeting the annual goals will be measured. [34 CFR §300.320(a)(3)(i)]

- When periodic reports on the progress the child is making toward meeting the annual goals will be provided, such as through the use of quarterly or other periodic reports, concurrent with the issuance of report cards. [34 CFR §300.320(a)(3)(ii)]

A statement of the <u>special education and related services</u> and supplementary aids and services, based on peer-reviewed research to the extent practicable, to be provided to the child, or on behalf of the child, and <u>a statement of the program modifications or supports</u> for school personnel that will be provided to enable the child:

- To advance appropriately toward attaining the annual goals. [34 CFR §300.320(a)(4)(i)]

- To be involved in and make progress in the general education curriculum and to participate in extracurricular and other nonacademic activities. [34 CFR §300.320(a)(4)(ii)]

- To be educated and participate with other children with disabilities and nondisabled children in extracurricular and other nonacademic activities. [34 CFR §300.320(a)(4)(iii)]

An explanation of the extent, if any, to which the child will not participate with nondisabled children in the regular classroom and in extracurricular and other nonacademic activities. [34 CFR §300.320(a)(5)]

(Continued)

Figure 1.1 (Continued)

A statement of any individual appropriate accommodations that are necessary to measure the academic achievement and functional performance of the child on State and districtwide assessments. [34 CFR §300.320(a)(6)(i)]

If the IEP Team determines that the child must take an alternate assessment instead of a particular regular State or districtwide assessment of student achievement, a statement of why:

- The child cannot participate in the regular assessment. [34 CFR §300.320(a)(6)(ii)(A)]

- The particular alternate assessment selected is appropriate for the child. [34 CFR §300.320(a)(6)(ii)(B)]

The projected date for the beginning of the services and modifications and the anticipated frequency, location, and duration of <u>special education and related services</u> and <u>supplementary aids and services and modifications and supports</u>. [34 CFR §300.320(a)(7)]

Service, Aid or Modification	Frequency	Location	Beginning Date	Duration

TRANSITION SERVICES

Beginning not later than the first IEP to be in effect <u>when the child turns 16, or younger if determined appropriate by the IEP Team</u>, and updated annually thereafter, the IEP must include:

- Appropriate measurable postsecondary goals based upon age-appropriate transition assessments related to training, education, employment, and where appropriate, independent living skills. [34 CFR §300.320(b)(1)]

- The transition services (including courses of study) needed to assist the child in reaching those goals. [34 CFR §300.320(b)(2)]

Transition Services (Including Courses of Study)

RIGHTS THAT TRANSFER AT AGE OF MAJORITY

- Beginning not later than one year before the child reaches the age of majority under State law, the IEP must include a statement that the child has been informed of the child's rights under Part B of the IDEA, if any, that will, consistent with 34 CFR §300.520, transfer to the child on reaching the age of majority. [34 CFR §300.320(c)]

As each snowflake is unique, so is each student, whether he or she is educated within an inclusive classroom or a self-contained setting. The needs of students on the special education continuum and within the general education classroom are heterogeneous ones. Even though students share a classification, they also share a commonality of diversity. As an example, students with autism are referred to as being on a spectrum since they display a wide variety of characteristics that include learning, communicative, behavioral, emotional, sensory, and social needs; accordingly, educators will need a variety of strategies. Activity schedules help with transition issues (Banda, Grimmett, & Hart, 2009). Strategies also include picture exchange communication systems, social stories, discrete trial training, explicit instruction, and other visual supports (Ryan, Hughes, Katsiyannis, McDaniel, & Sprinkle, 2011). This also includes capitalizing on student strengths, improving eye contact, helping students display social reciprocity, and finding ways to increase attention to areas outside focused interests. Continually researching available technology is also important, such as infusing a program such as *GoTalk* or *TouchChat* if the student uses an iPad instead of his or her natural voice to communicate.

COMMUNICATING THE STUDENT SPECTRUM TO YOUR STAFF

The rainbow of student characteristics needs to be acknowledged and matched with a continuum of services. Students with a specific learning disability (SLD) comprise a category under IDEA, but these learners are individual students who can be excellent readers, mathematicians, and writers who exhibit a combination of stronger and weaker skills with numeracy, literacy, organization, perceptual skills, and more. A student with a reading difference such as dyslexia does not automatically earn the additional label of dysgraphia or dyscalculia or any combination of assumed learning skills or weaknesses.

A student with an intellectual disability may have weaker expressive skills, but stronger receptive language skills that need to be honored and capitalized on. Some students need additional time to practice and recall information learned due to memory weaknesses (Nolet & McLaughlin, 2005) or additional verbal cues to generalize concepts learned from one situation to the next. Students who are deaf may use sign language, lip reading, oral language, and/ or total communication, while some students and their families prefer one mode of communication to another. A student with ADHD may exhibit one or all of the traits of inattentiveness, impulsivity, and hyperactivity. Students with emotional differences have internalizing and more passive behaviors such as depression or externalizing behaviors with more acting out, anger, or aggression displayed. Students with the label of Other Health Impairment (OHI) are a diverse group who may have attention issues, medical or physical concerns, and other characteristics. A student with a traumatic brain injury (TBI) may have mild, moderate, or severe implications with varying degrees of concentration, attention, thinking, motor impairments, or fatigue evidenced. A student with a visual impairment may be partially sighted, have low vision, or be totally blind, thereby requiring a combination of supports and services. Each and every inclusive classroom therefore presents students who have a spectrum of stronger and weaker skills, whether students are classified as gifted, twice exceptional, or one of the 13 disability categories under IDEA.

Overall, students who learn within inclusive classrooms share similar disability labels, but educators and staff need to view each student as an individual who possesses a unique personality with a spectrum of needs. In addition, the students who are peers of students with disabilities need to be sensitive to their classmates who have differing skills and levels. Students with classifications also need to realize that it is not always about them, but they too coexist within that classroom, sharing teachers' and teacher assistants' attention. No one student trumps the other one or justifies sacrificing instructional time since he or she possesses a lower or higher level of learning or behavioral needs. Teachers need to honor students' IEP requirements, but they also honor the integrity of each learner. Diversity exists within each group, whether one belongs to a theater club, a gym, a teacher's union, or a book club. Leaders help students, educators, and families understand and propagate this point to assist all students in growing up to be caring and productive adults who are able to capitalize on one another's uniqueness without judging one or the other as better or inferior. All students are worthy of life's fruitful experiences as adults.

Inclusion Coaching Roles and Partnerships

Inclusion coaches are catalysts who jump-start educators with innovative ideas as supportive, yet nonthreatening, collaborative agents of change. Coaching, an effective instructional model, propagates appropriate support systems to ensure that classrooms are welcoming ones that are set up to help educators and their students succeed (Davis, 2008). This includes unified systems of support from administration with formal times for collaborative teams to meet, discuss, and continually plan together. Administrators who make use of coaches allow their staff opportunities to collaboratively investigate how to continually teach, reach, and *include* learners of all ability levels. Coaches respond to educators' needs to meet teachers where they are through equitable partnerships, dialogue, and ongoing collaborations (Knight, 2007). Coaches act as multipliers and master teachers who inspire the capacity of others (Wiseman, 2010).

Administration, inclusion coaches, educators, and all related staff need to collaboratively address these foundational questions:

1. What types of assistance and coaching models are available, and which are favorable ones for the staff (e.g., principals leading, team/grade leaders, supervisors or administration organizing structure, co-teachers meeting collaboratively, related staff rotating responsibilities, outside consultants)?

2. How will the planning, instruction, and assessments be determined, shared, and evaluated before, during, and after the lessons/units and at regularly determined time intervals (e.g., each quarter, month, week, day)?

3. How can teachers and all staff regularly coach each other with support systems that value the efficacy, skills, and integrity of educators, students, families, administrators, the curriculum standards, and ongoing professional development?

Figure 2.1 delineates the many factors involved that inclusion coaches, teacher leaders, principals, supervisors, and all inclusive stakeholders collaboratively review.

Figure 2.1 Inclusion Coaching Checklist

For: Principals, Supervisors, Team and Grade-Level Leaders, Mentors, Instructional Coaches, Special Education and General Education Educators, Related Staff

School: Grades: Date:

Do we ...	Yes	Sometimes	*Rarely/ Never or N/A*	*Inclusion Improvement Plan*
A. Communication With Inclusive Staff				
A1. Communicate Direction and Decision-Making Processes				
1. Communicate on a regular basis what the school's needs are and what steps are needed to make changes to improve inclusive classrooms?				
2. Communicate inclusion priorities (e.g., inform staff of upcoming class lists and share IEPs)?				
3. Communicate often and clearly that change for inclusive improvements is not optional?				
4. Communicate planned partnerships and connections with the community (e.g., families are contacted with positive news as well as struggles)?				
5. Communicate the reasons for decisions (e.g., adaptations are IEP driven, co-teaching assignments)?				
6. Have an open-door policy to share concerns and ideas to talk about inclusion programs, lessons, and student concerns?				
7. Inform teachers on how their input will be used to further inclusive improvements for students, families, and staff?				
8. Provide clear and detailed information about the short- and long-term goals of the turnaround process (e.g., anticipated inclusion accomplishments by the end of the second marking period)?				
9. Model, encourage, and share the data to guide decisions?				
A2. Guide and Encourage Inclusive Staff				
1. Reassure teachers that anxiety, as part of a turnaround process, is a natural and very common response and work with teachers to overcome apprehensions or doubts about inclusive scenarios?				

Do we ...	Yes	Sometimes	Rarely/ Never or N/A	Inclusion Improvement Plan
2. Set clear expectations and visions for staff regarding inclusion programs and interventions?				
3. Set clear expectations for interpersonal interaction of staff with co-teachers, instructional assistants, team members, related staff, students, and families?				
4. Use multiple modes of communication to guide and encourage staff (e.g., attendance and support at IEP conferences, grade-level team meetings, GE/SE collaboration, and e-mails)?				
A3. Use Multiple Channels of Communication				
1. Use supervisors, department chairs, coaches, and team leaders to help collect and disseminate data?				
2. Use shared leadership practices (e.g., establish student support teams)?				
3. Find regular forums and creative ways to recognize staff for their inclusive achievements?				
4. Provide a safe environment in which teachers can collaborate about problems or challenges they are having with students, other staff members, and/or families?				
B. Instructional Inclusive Leadership				
B1. Observe, Model, and Co-Teach				
1. Observe instruction and interact with teachers and students?				
2. Model instructional/research-based inclusive strategies in the classroom?				
3. Create observational tools and inclusion documentation forms to assess alignment of instruction with interventions to access the CCSS?				
4. Serve as a role model for inclusive teaching, support strategies, and co-teaching practices?				
B2. Support Professional Development and Growth Opportunities				
5. Join together in professional development seminars and workshops about disabilities and instructional practices?				
6. Expand knowledge by attending training outside school and consulting with outside experts in the GE and SE fields, and then share the knowledge with all staff?				

(Continued)

Figure 2.1 (Continued)

Do we …	Yes	Sometimes	Rarely/ Never or N/A	Inclusion Improvement Plan
7. Plan and support professional staff development on disabilities and effective inclusion interventions?				
8. Incorporate research-based strategies into professional development (e.g., providing articles in journals such as *Teaching Exceptional Children*; inviting experts in the field; providing resources to staff [http://www.nichcy.org/, http://dww.ed.gov/, http://www.cast.org/])?				
9. Track staff professional inclusion growth and discuss professional development opportunities with all GE and SE staff?				
10. Encourage an environment of collaborative inquiry and ongoing inclusion planning?				
11. Encourage teachers to use evidence-based instructional practices in their inclusive classrooms?				
12. Initiate discussions with teachers about indicators for inclusion success and how to measure student academic and behavioral progress (e.g., RTI behavioral improvement plans)?				
13. Initiate discussion regarding students' grades in inclusive classrooms and graduation requirements?				
C. Connections With Inclusive Stakeholders				
1. Work to identify key stakeholders in communities that can be inclusion partners and allies?				
2. Conduct regular meetings with families and/or members of the community to explain inclusion and SE/GE goals and processes?				
3. Regularly inform families about the legislation, school priorities, and other policies?				
4. Propose and provide multiple opportunities to families and local businesses and organizations to contribute insights, time, and expertise?				
5. Collect data from families and community members for inclusive decision making and ongoing collaborations—in addition to IEP meetings?				

Do we ...	Yes	Sometimes	Rarely/ Never or N/A	Inclusion Improvement Plan
6. Inform families and community members how their input was or will be used for inclusive school improvements?				
7. Find out how the school can contribute to families and the community (e.g., by conducting family nights to provide training in effective literacy, math, or study skill strategies)?				
8. Find regular forums and creative ways to recognize families and community members for their contribution to the students' inclusive classrooms?				
9. Support mechanisms in the school that enable ongoing communication between the school and the community (e.g., SE/ GE parent support organizations and initiatives)?				

Source: Adapted from *School principal self-reflection: Leadership strategies.* Available from http://www.opi.mt.gov/streamer/profdev/ Supporting_Documents/Essential_3/Low-Performing/Handout13_ImprovedLeadership_SelfReflection_Principal.pdf

Administrative support (Billingsley, 2007) with resources and time is essential. It is one thing to verbally say, "Yes, more collaborative planning time is needed," but putting that plan into action then gains much inclusion mileage. Inclusion coaches continually facilitate ongoing discussions, reflections, and collaboration to strengthen co-teaching partnerships, instructional interventions, students' achievements of core curriculum standards, progress monitoring, and professional development. Together, different building levels of support are put into place. School leaders such as principals, directors, and curriculum supervisors communicate with coaches, teacher leaders, and mentors who then in turn have ongoing communications with educators and related staff. It is important that although there are levels of support in place, this support not be portrayed as a hierarchical structure that devalues any stakeholder's input. Collaboration is essential, with all parties accepting of each other's equitable voices.

Inclusion coaches offer ideas based on both educator and student levels and needs. In today's inclusion classrooms, educators plan lessons that have high expectations for all students. This requires matching the curriculum with the appropriate research-based instructional interventions (Kretlow & Blatz, 2011). Teachers require more awareness, professional support, structure, and reflections from inclusion coaches to decide on the research-based paths that will achieve those positive outcomes. Topics reviewed on What Works Clearinghouse (U.S. Department of Education, Institute of Education Sciences, n.d.), ranging from academic achievement to literacy, math interventions, student behavior, technology, and dropout prevention, need to be interpreted to thrive inside inclusive classrooms.

Now, just what does an inclusion coaching model look like? During inclusion coaching sessions, educators have shared a gamut of emotions, ranging from an exclamation such as "I love inclusion!" to a question such as "Why do I have to do inclusion?" Inclusion is still a controversial issue that has many administrators, school data support teams, educators, and families debating the merits of one program or service over another or making decisions over appropriate instructional supports or modalities (Armstrong, Armstrong, & Spandagou, 2011; Fialka, 2005). Inclusion in an Illinois classroom does not mirror inclusion in a Texas, New York City, Montreal, or Singapore classroom. Often, you can travel a radius of 15 miles in the same state, province, or region and witness five different types of inclusion classrooms with combinations of supports and labels such as full inclusion, in-class support, resource, replacement, and more. In addition to the legislative requirements, inclusive staff need to be aware of their students' interests. Preparation for adult life includes students studying subjects that match their talents, passions, and aspirations (Wiggins, 2011). It is imperative that coaches and teachers harmoniously work together to achieve student goals (Sweeney, 2009).

Although each inclusion classroom presents unique dynamics, here are eight coaching commonalities *to include.*

An inclusion coach

1. solicits input from administration, teams of teachers, and related staff to collaboratively formulate organizational frameworks, curricular plans, differentiated lessons, appropriate support systems, and progress monitoring;

2. observes classroom dynamics and listens to teachers without judging or evaluating them;

3. believes in educators' and students' successes;

4. focuses on students' individual needs while considering classroom dynamics and the subject content;

5. highlights the merits of applying learning and strategies received from professional development sessions;

6. continually researches, learns, and shares inclusion strategies;

7. builds trusting relationships with administration, team leaders, GE and SE teachers, related staff, families, and students; and

8. fosters a view of inclusion as an evolutionary process.

Now applying these eight coaching strategies is a task that is not to be viewed as one that befits Sisyphus. Negativity exists, but if positive inclusion coaching attitudes are shared, everyone is an inclusive winner.

Administrators, educators, and staff in inclusive classrooms need to continually and collaboratively

- analyze current levels of student performance;
- review curriculum standards, IEPs of students, intervention plans, and data;
- map annual, quarterly, monthly, weekly, and/or daily inclusion goals;
- design lessons and units of study that are shared with students and families;
- determine degree, timing, and intensity of inclusion strategies;
- apply and review appropriate accommodations and/or modifications;
- develop classroom management procedures for whole class, small group, and individual student instruction;
- evaluate and tweak lesson deliveries;
- network with each other;

- communicate data and progress to each other, students, and families;
- collaboratively plan, organize, and develop additional learning opportunities; and
- respectfully listen to each other.

Figure 2.2 highlights inclusion coaching classroom considerations using a middle school science classroom as an example. The chart is intended to record information to promote organized discussion for inclusion coaches, administrators, educators, and related staff. Its purpose will vary depending on whether the responses are generated during a coaching visit, one-on-one planning session, co-teacher debriefing, team meeting, administrative planning session, and more.

Figure 2.2   Inclusion Coaching Notes: Sample Lesson

Inclusion Coaching Notes		
Date: April 15	**Time:** Periods 6 and 7	**Room:** 102/Library
Co-Teachers: J and P		
a. **Classroom visit** b. Modeling/demo c. Related staff consult	d. One-on-one planning e. **Co-teacher debriefing** f. Instructional assistants	g. Reflection/follow-up meeting h. Content teachers/team meeting i. Administration planning
Subject: Life Science	**Unit:** Cells and Energy	**Concept:** Photosynthesis
Objective: To compare and contrast photosynthesis and respiration		

Lesson description: motivators, materials, instruction, guided practice, modeling, assessments, closure . . .

Do Now asked students to:

1. Write the formula for photosynthesis.

2. Write the formula for respiration.

3. Share similar traits of the two formulas.

- Structured learning environment focused students on task with the agenda and objectives posted. It was evident that this structure was nonnegotiable and ongoing.
- Great that the students came up to the board to write their responses to the *Do Now,* since it increased class involvement and offered more student recognition.
- Demanded academic vocabulary—*not that thing!*
- Excellent connections to students' lives with prior and upcoming lessons (e.g., edible cells, diffusion, genetics).
- Lesson closure: J asked, "What did you learn?" Each student contributed the knowledge he or she gained with responses that indicated learning strides.

Co-teaching models observed . . .

Lead-assist varied, with J and P alternately circulating to offer increased proximity to focus students and to ensure organization (e.g., J reviewed students' notes reminding them to place dates on papers and clearly label work; P and J continually probed students for on-target responses; lesson conversation was shared by the two teachers who seamlessly bounced ideas off each other as students joined discussions).

(Continued)

Figure 2.2   (Continued)

Student behaviors, response to interventions, accommodations, modifications . . .

17 students; all students were attentive, involved, and engaged within parameters that had clear expectations defined; prior knowledge was revealed with questioning (e.g., why drinking too much soda is not healthy);

students were responsive to co-teachers' ongoing higher-level questioning and monitoring; receptive to teacher praise and constructive feedback during whole class and independent work.

Classroom layout . . .

4–5 students at each lab table. Each teacher had a separate work area.

Recommendations . . .

- Invite students to generate a Venn diagram or three-column chart in their notebooks for photosynthesis and respiration comparison to visually compartmentalize their thoughts.
- Teach students to use the book's tools (e.g., instead of telling the page number where the formula is located, instruct students to use the index to find it).
- Vary co-teaching with a parallel model to divide the class to lower the student-teacher ratio during the *Do Now* or lesson (e.g., P reviews photosynthesis formula with one group, while J reviews respiration with the other half of the class, and then either the teachers or students physically switch).
- Connect with English language arts (e.g., teach word structure: *photo* [light] *synthesis* [putting together]).
- Kinesthetic exit cards (e.g., *snowball fight* to add written and kinesthetic components).
- Visual timeline of year's objectives with Common Core State Standards posted that highlights yearlong units of study.
- Share objectives with students with weekly calendars.
- Have an ongoing center with approximately 10 minutes each week devoted to other science topics that interest the students (e.g., *What I saw on the Discovery Channel*) to structure the tangential moments.

Questions to resolve . . .

Varying and infusing other co-teaching models in each lesson

Revisiting lessons and concepts to encourage retention

Additional comments and feedback . . .

Several classified students were out on a trip or absent—different class dynamics on those days.

Online resources . . .

Flashcards, tests, and more: http://quizlet.com/3664088/test/

http://quizlet.com/4297421/genetics-the-science-of-heredity-flash-cards/

Excellent questions and activities could be generated from charts accessed at: http://www.vtaide.com/png/photosynthesis.htm

---

Revisitation plans: Inclusion resources, strategies, and lesson plans will be collaboratively reviewed in weekly team meetings and upcoming coaching sessions.

Summer professional development days to map quarterly units

Open invite to e-mail questions: toby@inclusionworkshops.com

Source: © Toby Karten, 2012

Figure 2.3 invites inclusion coaches to organize and share thoughts with educators during debriefing sessions.

Figure 2.3 Inclusion Coaching Notes: Template

Inclusion Coaching Notes		
Date(s): **Time:** **Period:** **Room:**		

Teachers/Staff:

a. Classroom visit
b. Modeling/demo
c. Related staff consult

d. One-on-one planning
e. Co-teacher debriefing
f. Instructional assistants

g. Reflection/follow-up
    meeting
h. Content teachers/team
    meeting
i. Administration planning

Subject:	**Unit:**	**Concept:**

Objective/Common Core State Standards:

Lesson description: motivators, materials, instruction, guided practice, modeling, assessments, closure . . .

Co-teaching model(s) (if applicable) . . .

Student behaviors, response to interventions, accommodations, modifications . . .

Classroom layout . . .

Recommendations . . .

Questions to resolve . . .

Additional comments and feedback . . .

Revisitation plans . . .

RESPECTFUL ADMINISTRATION
FOR INCLUSIVE SCHOOLS

Inclusion begins from the top down and often laterally as well since collaboration is a nonnegotiable inclusive ingredient. Administrators support the coaching process with concrete steps that break down inclusion barriers by respecting collaborative input. Principals influence teacher actions in the classroom and in turn student achievements (DuFour & Marzano, 2011). It is essential that principals, administrators, supervisors, and all school leaders offer guidance and ongoing support to their staff to foster the effective use of collaboration skills and the many special education scenarios they confront (Angelle & Bilton, 2009; Hines, 2008). More reforms are evidenced when teachers in inclusive environments work together to reach common goals for their students (Brownell, Adams, Sindelar, Waldron, & Vanhover, 2006). With administrative support, general and special educators, co-teaching teams, and related staff conduct ongoing discussions, reflections, and collaborations to plan, implement, and document students' responses to inclusion interventions through formative assessments. Research on using formative assessments affirms the learning benefits (Black & William, 1998; Weurlander, Soderberg, Scheja, Hult, & Wernerson, 2012).

Superintendents, school boards, and other school leaders scrutinize and review existing and new programs and services to determine which ones to introduce, continue, or change. These four tips are offered to measure the effectiveness of programs and strategies:

1. Use controlled experiments.

2. Determine the reason for successful programs.

3. Offer common formative assessments.

4. Abandon programs with zero returns (Levenson, 2011).

Levenson (2011) uses an example that compares resource and co-taught programs in one school district. This researcher mentions that students' English and math gains were achieved at the same rate in both settings and goes on to say that since the resource or *pullout* setting is less expensive than the co-taught or *push-in* program, the district might consider reallocating its programming to have more students pulled out. That may be a wise cost-effective decision for this school district, but school leaders need to also look at the bigger inclusive picture to determine if it is an appropriate decision. Other factors may be involved, such as students having lower self-esteem when they are pulled out of the general education classroom, the presence of less peer modeling and fewer social interactions, the depth and breadth of the curriculum, and whether all special education co-teachers and resource teachers have the same expertise as the general education teachers. Determining if this is a norm and whether the same results would be achieved over longer amounts of time is essential. In addition, each student's program needs to be investigated on an individual basis, or dangerous legislative precedents could arise if administrators make decisions solely based on dollar amounts. Again, the many variables present involve collaborative scrutiny to decide on programs that achieve the best results. Everyone agrees that it is important to maximize achievements for students with special needs, but determining how to wisely use the resources is never a uniform administrative decision due to the unique abilities of each student.

A school leader or principal has a variety of roles that involve much more than being the decision maker who determines the hiring, firing, and evaluating of his or her staff. The school leader is often simultaneously a communicator, negotiator, facilitator, collaborator, coach, and juggler of all. These roles involve assisting educators and related staff along with students and their families to figure out how to obtain effective results for students who are educated within inclusive classrooms. The *Principal Quality Practice Guideline* from Alberta Education (2009) lists a principal's role as fostering effective relationships, embodying visionary leadership, providing instructional leadership, developing and facilitating leadership, managing school operations and resources, and understanding and responding to larger societal context. Good leadership recognizes the capacity within a school culture to value and support the learning. This changes the decision making into a consultative and collaborative process. Good leaders nurture and affirm team-building activities and the concept of shared and respectful leadership.

Today, the school leadership role is not an autocratic one, but one that respects and values all integral and collaborative players. The U.S. government now has a project titled RESPECT:

R ecognizing

E ducational

S uccess

P rofessional

E xcellence

and

C ollaborative

T eaching

This project aims to transform the profession by involving and respecting teachers, leaders, associations, and unions on district, state, and national levels. It envisions the teaching profession to be led by teachers since at times there are degrees of disconnect between reality and practice. It hopes to attract top-tier talent to the field, look at how teachers are evaluated and supported in meaningful ways, allow the best teachers to help the most needy students, and offer the conditions for teachers to succeed with a national model and mentors. The RESPECT Project seeks to transform the profession by honoring teacher input and experiences. Principals and school leaders allow master teachers to be their collaborative partners. Teachers would serve as mentors who are given the time and resources to share their expertise. This project, in its infancy at the time of this publication, holds promise for the teaching profession to be identified and looked upon with respect and for students who are educated in inclusive classrooms to receive the expertise of highly recognized staff. For more information see Brenchley (2012).

In addition to recognizing their staff's strengths, principals need to be highly visible to connect with students, families, communities, and the leaning process (Ryan, 2012). The student relationships forged build children's self-esteem in a nurturing yet structured environment. Students with disabilities too often concentrate on what they are doing wrong or need to improve upon. When a principal or school leader offers learners with differences positive recognition, whether a smile or an official award, it increases student self-efficacy. Slating time each day to gather data and deal with budget issues is part of a principal and school leader's job, but devoting time to visit inclusion classrooms for productive formal and informal visits to recognize the arduous efforts of both educators and students is also vital.

Time is also often an issue, since there never seems to be a schedule that everyone on the staff simultaneously embraces. Principals who formulate inclusion class schedules must consider how to build in common planning time for co-teachers and all related staff to continually ensure that the instruction matches individual student and class needs throughout the year. Time for professional and collaborative development to support teacher-led teams is a vital component. The data offer valuable information for teams to review to drive instructional decisions. Educators analyze the data, reflect on current practices, and formulate action plans that use the data in a meaningful way (Wellman & Lipton, 2003). Some ways to schedule collaborative team planning time is with approaches such as offering extra prep periods, shared classes, and extended time to collaborate and review the data during faculty meetings and scheduled professional development days, or early release times. This allows for increased collaboration beyond the regularly scheduled preps, which often are spent returning parent phone calls, copying student worksheets for the next day's lesson, and other assorted noncollaborative but imperative tasks.

In addition, inviting input from co-teachers and assistants on whom they want to work with and student assignments is essential. Asking staff for their top three assignment wishes builds in both flexibility and empowerment. It honors staff input and offers administrators a range of options. Starting the year off on this positive note then benefits everyone.

Time well spent also includes connecting with families and community supports. Setting up monthly community or family co-led meetings and communicating that all input is invited is a proactive way to ensure that communication and supports are ongoing. Families who are allowed to express their disagreements are then able to partner with the schools to find out more about inclusive programs on topics ranging from helping with homework to family support of a behavioral plan.

Productive and pragmatic principals realize that inclusive environments are not built on their shoulders alone but involve respecting and collaborating with students, their families, general and special education staff, community members, and all integral inclusive stakeholders. Administrators are the key players who set the stage for ongoing professional collaboration to achieve better student outcomes.

COLLABORATIVE LEARNING SUPPORT TEAMS AND TEACHER LEADERSHIP

"Within every school there is a sleeping giant of teacher leadership, which can be a strong catalyst for making change" (Katzenmeyer & Moller, 2001). Teachers need to teach and coach each other, not just their students. The configuration of collaborative learning support teams varies with a range that includes coaches, mentors, grade-level leaders, supervisors, curriculum directors, professional learning communities, and other staff who facilitate ongoing dialogue to make integral decisions. These teams may be student-centered or curriculum-driven, or review instructional support, data, and effective interventions and assessments. Teams investigate inclusion strategies, instructional practices, student literacy and mathematics levels, family concerns, and more.

The facilitators who guide these groups include a variety of professionals, such as school principals, curriculum supervisors, behavioral interventionists, learning consultants, instructional coaches, seasoned staff members, co-teachers, grade leaders, mentor- or master-level teachers, and other staff. Together these individuals formulate inclusion plans with appropriate goals that focus on high learning outcomes for students who are taught within the general education classroom. Collaborative support teams focus on how to increase student strengths, rather than magnifying student deficits. It is no longer a question that all students can learn, but the query is how the learning will occur. Supports and resources that facilitators offer to educators and students include a range of academic, financial, and emotional ones.

Talking out ideas with colleagues who offer nonevaluative input is invaluable in determining appropriate inclusive classroom setups. Meaningful conversations happen when trusting relationships are built (Brooks-Rallins, 2011). Collaboration yields significant achievement gains when teams of teachers are allocated sufficient time to work together (Saunders, Goldenberg, & Gallimore, 2009). Ongoing collaborative support translates children's individual education programs into realistic classroom practices that circumvent the limitations perceived, inferred, or assumed by student labels. Collaborative teams identify learning targets and design common unit tasks and assessment instruments (William, 2011). For example, the classroom-focused improvement process in Maryland has grade-level, cross-level, and vertical teacher teams focus on student achievements as an ongoing part of their lesson-planning cycle (Maryland State Department of Education, 2012). It values a step-by-step approach conducted with team inquiry that responds to student data. It reviews student patterns to make determinations on future instructional plans.

The Teacher Leadership Exploratory Consortium (2012) developed teacher model standards for experienced teachers to assume leadership roles such as instructional specialists, mentors, facilitators, and school team leaders (Harrison & Killion, 2007). Capitalizing on the expertise within a staff values school improvement. This inclusive culture validates and expands staff roles, responsibilities, perspectives, and the expertise of all to strengthen student achievements. Standard 3 of the Interstate School Leaders Licensure Consortium (ISLLC) Standards (School Administration Publishing, 2012) states that an education leader promotes the success of every student by ensuring effective management of the organization, operation, and resources for a safe, efficient, and effective learning environment. Principals who are able to reorganize their own thinking to recognize staff strengths and share leadership within collaborative groups of teachers are then multiplying the learning for both teachers and students.

EDUCATORS AND RELATED STAFF

This broad pedagogical cast of characters includes, but is not limited to, general educators; special educators; co-teachers; support teachers; resource teachers; instructional assistants; one-on-one educational aides; speech-language pathologists; behavioral, occupational, and physical therapists; mobility trainers; teachers of the deaf; teachers of students with visual impairments; and art, music, dance, physical education, health, language, library, guidance, and technology teachers. Depending on what is stated in students' IEPs in reference to frequency, location, and duration, the SE services given may be within the GE classroom for all of the day, part of the day or class period, or none of the day. If a student is not educated within the GE setting, then reasons that the GE setting is not appropriate must be delineated in that student's IEP. Educators who teach students outside of the GE classroom for part or all of the day also benefit from the collaborative knowledge that inclusion coaching offers. Visiting one another's classrooms offers ideas for improving inclusion management, instructional strategies, and co-teaching practices. When related staff such as speech therapists collaborate with teachers in the GE classroom, then students reap the benefits of increased modeling and more exposure to the academic content alongside their peers, instead of being pulled out for the specialized services. This necessitates the formulating and sharing of lessons and all parties being given common planning time to decide lesson content and instructional approaches. It also means that teachers and other staff are flexible enough to realize that one person does not own the inclusion answers but that solutions are collaboratively designed based on student and class needs and curriculum concerns.

It is also the responsibility of educators to think beyond *what* is taught, to *how* a subject, concept, topic, or skill is taught and *to whom*. Everyone needs to be on board with the knowledge and skills to ensure that if a child is placed within an inclusive GE classroom, then the appropriate classroom structure, supports, and scaffoldings are in place. The idea is not to sacrifice one group for the next, but to address whole class, small group, and individual student differences. This includes the implementation of proactive approaches such as universal design for learning (UDL) and RTI, with the knowledge of these practices offered to the general education staff with all collaborative personnel on board. Staff need to understand that UDL allows teachers to vary the planning, instruction, and assessments with proactive approaches that value student differences with aligned goals, materials, lessons, and assessments. The Center for Applied Special Technology (CAST, 2012) offers excellent resources that help inclusive partners to continually review the ways that students are engaged in the learning. For a video offering an overview of UDL principles, visit the National Center on Universal Design for Learning, at CAST (2012). School leaders and coaches can share these UDL resources with staff.

RTI allows the assessments to truly be formative ones that modify and drive instruction for all students. Students with disabilities or special educators do not own RTI, but it falls under the responsibilities of all staff before a diagnosis of a specific learning disability is given. Figure 2.4 invites team leaders, educators, and coaches to collaboratively review whole-class, small-group, and individual student RTIs at set time periods during each marking period.

Educator training and allotting time for collaboration, along with emotional and financial support to deliver lessons with differentiated goals, methods, materials, and assessments, are part of the inclusive equation. For an example, deciding if an inclusion coaching meeting will take place every four to six weeks, twice a month for one hour each session, or on a weekly basis for 30–40 minutes to review a form such as Figure 2.4 is a collaborative decision that educators and administrators formulate and agree upon. In addition, allowing the meetings to be held during the course of the school day values educators' time and efforts, rather than imposing educator attendance at meetings that often occur at everyone's least productive times—after school, when an entire day of teaching has preceded the meeting.

CO-TEACHING RESPONSIBILITIES

Collaboration within the inclusive environment often includes implementing effective co-teaching practices. Co-teaching is often compared to a marriage, with professionals working side by side. Some of the challenges include identifying roles and responsibilities, figuring out times to plan, and deciding on co-teaching structures or approaches for each lesson. Some options include supportive, parallel, complementary, and team teaching (Villa, Thousand, & Nevin, 2010). One teacher can take the lead, while another educator monitors students, rotates around to observe, records data, offers closer proximity to keep students on task, and generally assists with whatever is needed. The class can also be divided into two parallel heterogeneous groups while co-teachers simultaneously instruct groups of

Figure 2.4 Response to Intervention (RTI) Form

Intervention Plans and Reflections for Students and Subject(s):		
Marking Period:	Week(s):	Dates:
(WC) Whole class comments:		
(SG) Small group comments:		
(1:1) Individualized, one-to-one comments:		
Parallel activity needed for these students:		
Roles/concerns/support of:		
General educator:		
Special educator:		
Instructional assistants/paraprofessionals:		
Instructional support teams:		
Related services:		
Administration:		
Family/home:		
Peers:		
Guidance counselor:		
Other reflections/support:		

Source: Karten, T. (2011). *Inclusion lesson plan book for the 21st century* (Teacher training edition). Port Chester, NY: Dude Publishing. Used with permission.

students on different or related lessons. For example, in a social studies class one teacher can give a mini lesson on primary sources, while the other co-teacher reviews secondary sources. A science lesson might involve smaller groups of students receiving instruction on subtopics such as gravity or inertia. Math co-teachers may instruct two groups of students separately on how to express a ratio as a fraction or a decimal. Perhaps an English class has each teacher instructing separate groups of students on different approaches to revising an essay. The students then switch teachers and groups to receive instruction on all topics. Teachers also co-teach as a team, bouncing ideas off each other to promote more modeling and class discussion. If centers or stations are set up, then co-teachers and educational assistants rotate around the classroom to work with smaller groups or individual students to lower the class ratio of teacher to students, offering time for remediation and/or enrichment.

Co-teaching models offer educators the opportunity to work with the class as a whole group, smaller groups of learners, and individual students. Classroom learning stations, cooperative assignments, and consultative services are a few ways that general and special educators collaborate to help students to achieve academic, social, emotional, behavioral, perceptual, and communicative goals. Co-teachers also often guide the roles for related staff providers, paraprofessionals, and peers within the classrooms. The best scenarios exist when both co-teachers rotate models and share all roles and responsibilities, from planning to instruction and assessments. Co-teaching partners who model respect and offer credibility to each other offer each other strong collaborative relationships, which are then transferred to students' successes. In the past, the general educator was viewed as the keeper of the knowledge, while the special educator was considered the gatekeeper of the strategies. Today, that is no longer the case. Many preservice education programs offer dual certification for a degree in both general and special education. Today, to be an effective co-teacher, it is crucial to have a handle on both the characteristics of learners and the subjects taught, whether you are considered to be a general or a special educator.

Parity of roles and responsibilities is healthy for all co-teaching relationships (Friend & Cook, 2009). The overall objective of co-teaching is to advance students' levels, without stepping on each other's toes, but somehow synchronizing a dance. Challenges exist when the music keeps changing and the partners keep rotating, or if one teacher thinks he or she is the one who must always lead. Again, inclusion is a process with no definitive answers, since the definitive student does not exist. Unique situations with learners, scheduling and class structures, attitudes, and co-teaching models need to be defined in each school setting to identify and apply the appropriate strategies and interventions. Figures 2.5 and 2.6 are offered to assist co-teachers to reflectively think about the benefits and challenges of different co-teaching models and the application of these models to their inclusive classrooms. Inclusion coaches encourage educators to collaboratively discuss and apply models that appropriately match each inclusion setting.

Figure 2.5 Benefits and Challenges of Co-Teaching Models

Co-Teaching Models	Benefits	Challenges
Bouncing ideas off each other	Fresh perspectives, more accountability, better ideas, and additional creativity offered with multiple perspectives, expertise, and connections shared, keeping the class together as a whole. Excellent modeling of thought processes through dialogue.	Clashing personalities, time constraints, and different viewpoints with too many disorganized, off-task ideas or distractions. Sometimes the teachers are too different or do not get along well enough to create solid discussions and plans. Knowledge base and grade-level experiences of each teacher vary.
Parallel teaching	Can easily teach to different strengths and present diverse ways to approach the same concept. Offers smaller class size management between two teachers. Allows for varying levels and multiple intelligences to be acknowledged, supported, and challenged more easily. Lowers student-teacher ratio by dividing the class into groups. Students enjoy hearing and seeing different perspectives and instructional approaches from adult voices.	One teacher overpowering the other teacher or assistant; often the special education teacher or assistant doesn't have the same content background as the general education teacher. Sometimes the teachers are not teaching the same thing at the same time, and the groups as a result are being adjusted, and one is falling behind the other group. Some students may be distracted by the noise level and simultaneous instruction if the parameters and expected student behavior during instruction and while switching groups are not clearly defined and managed.
One leading, one assisting	Clear differentiation of roles, depending on content knowledge and skills, better attention ratio. One teacher leads the classroom with a single focus, and allows the other teacher or support staff to study students and assist as needed with personal instruction, observation, recording of data, scaffolding, and classroom management.	Too much differentiation of teacher roles in front of the students may lead to power struggles. Power dynamic in the classroom is strictly defined; students may find the support teacher to be better than the leading teacher, and avoid listening to the leading teacher or the obverse. Assisting educator may resent the lead one and feel like a glorified helper rather than an equal partner, if lead-assist roles are not intermittently exchanged and supported.
Small groups, 1:1	Can work toward specific goals, better individual understandings with lower student-teacher ratio to focus on objectives. Micromanagement of classroom space and time allows for intimate intervention with the students, affording them the special attention that they may need in given lessons for remediation and or advancement.	Not integrated into a normal school setting, no peer interaction. Depends on the size of the groups. If the focusing is on 1:1, the problem is that students are not developing with peers as strongly as they would in a traditional classroom setting. May lead to stigmatization if group purpose and makeup are not varied for skills and subjects throughout the year.
Stations/centers	Working within groups on projects makes it easier to focus on an individual task or for a teacher to observe and inconspicuously assist a student as needed. Focus is on one task at a time with a teacher who is specialized. Students are cooperatively learning specific skills as collaborative peers. Individual student accountability can be built into stations.	Depending on the teachers in the classroom and the assignment, it may be difficult to keep up with the station work produced. Can limit the special attention to each group based on time given to earlier groups. May seem chaotic if structures with defined outcomes at stations and centers are not outlined with modeling and rubrics for academic, behavioral, social, and communicational expectations.
Consultation from team/related staff	Different strengths of staff are capitalized on with multiple perspectives, teaching techniques, and experiences. More feedback validates and expands inclusion strategies and interventions.	Some may claim that there are too many cooks in the kitchen. If the recommendations are based on one visit or observation, then the snapshot seen may not yield realistic recommendations. Needs ample time slotted for ongoing planning and communication.
Our thoughts, comments, and future actions		

Figure 2.6 Positive Co-Teaching Actions

Positive Co-Teaching Actions: *With your co-teacher, support staff, and/or collaborative teams, select three co-teaching actions that you think are the most important.*

a. Respect that you and your colleagues have personality differences and unique teaching styles, but remain firmly planted on *common classroom ground* that has positive students' outcomes as your collaborative goals.

b. Support co-teachers in front of other staff members, students, administration, and families.

c. Have a sense of humor and flexibility for situations, even the ones that defy all rules or expectations.

d. Be prepared to agree and/or disagree on any given day, remembering that it is vital to have ongoing communication.

e. Adapt course content together, grade together, laugh together, and know when to walk away from each other, too!

f. Decide ahead of time on acceptable adaptations for all students, not just those students with IEPs.

g. Vary your teaching styles: assisting, leading, or following one another's lead with shared lesson delivery during whole class, smaller group, or individualized instruction.

h. Be *two-faced,* which in this case means exchanging roles, allowing students to view each of you as equal partners, both worthy of the name *teacher.*

i. Share ideas with each other and other grade-level teachers and staff privately or in arranged meetings.

j. Be aware of the standards and course unit planning, but understand that pacing is not racing.

k. Focus on hearing each other, not just talking to each other. Definitely talk to each other in front of the students to stimulate more thinking skills.

l. Raise your own level of professional development by learning and practicing a new strategy each week, belonging to organizations, reading journals and magazines, learning more about students with different learning needs, observing other co-taught classes, and being open to new ideas.

m. Accept each other's needs, prior experiences, and future potential.

n. Give each other space, literally—classroom areas to work (e.g., desks, filing cabinets, bookshelves for resources)—and also mental space—time to digest, cool down, rethink, prioritize, and reflect.

o. Remember that you are both professionals who chose this job for reasons other than the lucrative financial gains!

p. Be aware of desirability vs. feasibility.

q. Like what you do, finding positive qualities in each other, your students, and life!

Source: Adapted from Karten, T. (2009). *Inclusion strategies that work for adolescent learners.* Thousand Oaks: CA: Corwin.

When educators delineate and share planning, instruction, and assessment responsibilities, then the educator-student ratio and the task load for each professional are lowered. As mentioned, there are several co-teaching models that educators infuse into an inclusion classroom. Together co-teachers and support staff alternate to lead or assist one another; instruct the whole class; teach parallel lessons simultaneously; work with individual students or smaller groups of students to enrich, reinforce, or reteach concepts or skills; circulate around to assist as needed during whole-class instruction; record data based on observations of student behavior; team-teach the same lesson; and more. There is no one co-teaching model that suits each classroom, all educator personalities, or all student needs, but varying the type of models implemented and responsibilities based on each inclusion classroom of students or subject taught is essential. Figure 2.7 is intended to invite educators and staff to continually reflect upon co-teaching model choices.

Figure 2.7   Reflecting on Our Co-Teaching Practices

Reflecting on Our Co-Teaching Practices

Collaboratively record co-teaching styles for 10 days, listing the approximate percentage of time you as co-teachers, support staff, and/or assistants practice these models each day. Then total each column and obtain a 10-day average for each model. Reflect on which ones you as a team want to practice more or less often. Additional comments are optional.

Dates	Team Teaching/ Bouncing Ideas Off Each Other	One Lead/ One Assist and Observe (Collecting or Recording Data)	Parallel Teaching	Small Groups/ 1:1	Stations/ Centers	Consultation/ Other Practice
1.						
2.						
3.						
4.						
5.						
6.						
7.						
8.						
9.						
10.						
Total (%)						
Average: Divide each column total by 10						
Comments (optional)						

Inclusive educators who co-teach need ongoing support with planning time, resources, communications, inclusive interventions, co-teaching models, shared instructional practices, and how to select appropriate lesson and assessment strategies. Collaborative input from inclusion coaching structures offers educators opportunities for confirmation, reflection, and encouragement.

FAMILY DYNAMICS

Source: Designed at Wordle (http://www.wordle.net).

Often families who have children with disabilities are at different levels of acceptance when it comes to their children's needs. Parental emotions include feelings that may involve a combination of guilt, denial, hostility, acceptance, and other negative and positive feelings. Emily Perl Kingsley, a screenwriter for *Sesame Street*, offers her perspective on what it is like to raise a child with a disability in her essay, *Welcome to Holland,* which was written in 1987 and inspired by her son who has Down syndrome. Her essay reminds of us of the many emotions a parent of a child with a disability experiences. Kingsley compares the experience to planning a fabulous trip to Italy and then finding out that the plane has landed in Holland instead. Once you discover the wonderful things about Holland, you then realize that the flight change, although an unexpected one, offers a world filled with tulips and Rembrandts, rather than gondolas and Michelangelos. Her essay can be accessed online (see Kingsley, 1987) and shared with administrators, educators, parents, and all school staff to gain more perspectives on and sensitivities to family dynamics. Administrators and team leaders also encourage families to be part of school parent groups or perhaps form their own forum to specifically share ideas with other parents and families who may be facing similar challenges. The following are three online resources among many available ones that leaders, coaches, and educators can investigate and share with families to offer more support:

Children's Disability List of Lists: http://www.comeunity.com/disability/speclists.html

Parents Helping Parents: www.php.com

Parent Support Groups for Children with Disabilities or Special Needs: http://www.childrensdisabilities.info/parenting/groups-childrensdisabilities.html

 Families and communities who are welcomed by educators with collaborative attitudes become protagonists who allow the learning to be continued beyond the school doors. When educators establish early positive relationships with families as partners, then students are the recipients of learning environments both at school and at home (Algozzine, Daunic, & Smith, 2010; Jeynes, 2005). The best scenarios occur when the line of communication between schools and homes is continually open. Educators also need to remember to share the good phone calls too, before they offer lists of what a student who is someone's son or daughter did wrong. Families sometimes need an ear to listen and offer objectivity, and cannot view administrators and educators as sole sources of criticism. Some families also need additional coaching to realize that the placement of their child in an inclusion class is not an automatic indicator of success, but that success requires ongoing positive student efforts and attitudes, and supportive partnering homes.

Educators who solicit and value family input gain more complete pictures of their students. Students sometimes display one type of behavior at home and a differing behavior at school. At times parents are advocates for their children, and at times educators assume that role as well. IEPs require family input with specific planning recommendations until students reach the age of majority at 18. Families need to be informed of their child's progress and be regularly updated at set time periods during the school year.

Often families are willing to partner with schools, but require specific guidance on how to help their children to achieve more knowledge and independence. For example, the SCERTS Model (2012) for students with autism advocates that parents be offered emotional and educational support to improve their confidence and ability levels to help their children and that educators also be offered support for challenging work-related situations (Prizant, Wetherby, Rubin, Laurent, & Rydell, 2003). The acronym focuses upon these crucial areas to increase learning and interactions:

SC Social-Communication

ER Emotional Regulation

TS Transactional Support (learning tools)

Encourage families to communicate valid input since quite often they know their children best, seeing them at different levels of performance. Together, schools and homes that coach and support each and every child multiply the learning experiences. Helping families with continued collaboration must be a priority for educators who can offer positive, proactive, and solution-oriented approaches (Edwards & Da Fonte, 2012).

Figure 2.8 is intended as a starting point for establishing healthy home-school partnerships. Both educators and families are invited to customize the

Figure 2.8 Family Collaborations: Proactive Approaches

At school, teachers will . . .	At home, families will . . .
Deliver whole-class, small-group, and individualized instruction	Talk to students about things that they are learning in school (e.g., monitor homework and long-range projects)
Share monthly lessons, units, themes, and strategies with families	Encourage students to review current lessons and topics and to preview upcoming assignments
Keep an ongoing line of communication open	Share all concerns with teachers as needs arise

chart and to continually add ideas. The intention is for each environment to agree upon a given set of responsibilities. Coaches and school leaders encourage educators to continually partner with families by establishing proactive roles and structures, as shown in Figure 2.8.

It is important that educators be encouraged to record their family contacts. Figure 2.9 reminds staff to continually document family contacts.

The National Dissemination Center for Children with Disabilities (NICHCY) offers excellent resources and organizations for families to access information (available in both English and Spanish) ranging from rights under IDEA to available services in communities and support groups (see NICHCY, n.d.).

Figure 2.9 Communication Logs

Communication Logs: E-mail/Phone/Meetings/Skype

Date(s) and type of contact, (e.g., phone, e-mail, conference)	Student	Name/ relationship of contact	Reasons for contact Remember to make the POSITIVE phone calls, too!	Details/outcomes/further follow-ups needed Positive, negative or neutral results achieved Further actions or recommendations required

Source: Karten. T. (2011). *Inclusion lesson plan book for the 21st century* (Teacher training edition). Port Chester, NY: Dude Publishing. Used with permission.

Connecting the Rules to Inclusion Coaching Strategies

"**S**o you are not here to rock our world!" It was an *aha* insight that an educator shared after a productive inclusion coaching session. It was only after that nonexample realization that a trusting coaching relationship was established. A coach offers reflective and worldly insights, never spinning a teacher's world into frenzy. A coach is not a spy, nor is a coach a person who offers a quick fix. A coach facilitates ongoing collaborative relationships that allow everyone to shine. There are some basic overarching inclusion rules that need to be viewed as everyday natural occurrences. The curriculum is never more important than the students who are learning the information. Nor is the professional development ever disconnected from the educators' everyday classroom scenarios. Overall, inclusion rules when ongoing professionalism, compassion, structure, awareness, and reflections occur within collaborative and trusting environments.

Be Professional

Professionalism creates, supports, and sustains school, district, and community-based inclusion. Coaches help people to think in new ways by facilitating dialogue and providing scaffolding, clear expectations, visions, and goals within respectful environments (Kee, Anderson, Dearing, Harris, & Schuster, 2010). Professional knowledge about inclusion strategies and students' abilities involves continuous and collaborative investigations by school staff beginning with day one and continuing throughout the year. Professional collaboration allows the educational climate to propagate student seeds of achievement. Special education and general education practices are linked to *include* all students, staff, and families. Inclusion cannot exist as a separate entity but must exist within the context of a school community that professionally structures, nurtures, and connects inclusive practices to co-teachers, related staff, administrators, students, and families. This includes the sharing and planning of goals and objectives with colleagues, students, and families. Education now allows students of all abilities access to the learning, but professionals who plan together also coach each other. Professional learning communities are supported by research, proven in practice, endorsed by professional organizations, and grounded in common sense (DuFour, DuFour, & Eaker, 2008). Inclusion coaching strategies need to be an integral part of school communities' agendas to offer educators appropriate inclusion supports and strategies. Inclusion is an integral part of professional development. Professionals honor core curriculum standards, inclusion strategies, students' abilities, and the value of realistic and trusting communications.

SMART GOALS TO INCLUDE

Professional learning communities advocate that goals are specific, measurable, attainable, realistic, and timely. *INCLUDE* goals offer the following parameters:

I ndividualize

N aturalize

C ollaborate

L earn

U nderstand

D ifferentiate

E valuate

Individualize

A teacher does not teach a class of 30 students, but instead he or she instructs each student in a class of 30. Within inclusive classrooms, students possess a variety of academic, communicative, sensory, developmental, physical, social, behavioral, perceptual, and emotional levels. Teachers who individualize their lessons appeal to different learners. For example, educators and staff offer more auditory opportunites to students with visual impairments and more visuals for students with hearing differences. Students with intellectual disabilites learn algebra when the steps are broken down and concrete manipulatives demonstrate and accompany the concepts. Teachers who allow students to learn the same material in different ways are setting the stage for many inclusive successes. Students do not learn at the same pace or level. Some students may require more repetition, while other students require more enrichment activities. Adaptations are student specific since each student is an individual learner who processes and retains information differently. This message is a clear and nonnegotiable one.

Naturalize

Quite often, attitude is the card that trumps successful inclusion programs. Research indicates that postive inclusion teacher mind-sets influence whether educators adapt their teaching methodology for students with varying learning needs (Cullen, Gregory, Jess, & Noto, 2010). While I was facilitating a parent panel, a mother communicated her wish for the *n* in the word *inclusion* to stand for the word *natural.* Educators and administrators need to wholeheartedly believe that inclusion is a natural way to educate students.

Collaborate

The purpose of inclusion teacher collaboration is to obtain improved student achievements (Brownell et al., 2006; Scruggs, Mastropieri, & McDuffie, 2007). Co- teachers, support staff, teams, coaches, administrators, general and special educators, and families who continually collaborate in and out of the classroom put aside personalities and concentrate on the students in a professional manner to review data, decide on appropriate programs, and monitor student progress. This is sometimes easier said than done and requires consistent efforts to happen. Co-teaching is compared to a marriage and requires the same diligence to achieve successful results, without *professional annulments!* Families also have varying emotions, concerns, and input that need to be validated and supported by the school staff. Ultimately, students and peers are the ones who collaborate with everyone, since without their voices and active involvement, there is no inclusion.

Learn

We need to learn *about* and *from* our students. Collaborative teams of professional learners consistently reflect on the following educational questions:

- What is it we want our students to learn?
- How will we know if each student has learned it?
- How will we respond when some students do not learn it?
- How can we extend and enrich learning for students who have demonstrated proficiency? (DuFour, DuFour, Eaker, & Many, 2006)

Inclusion communities of educators respond to these questions, with research-based inclusion strategies that reflect on students' and educators' strengths. This includes having high expectations for all students to learn.

Understand

No two students are the same, whether they are educated in an inclusion classroom or not. Linda Brandenburg, director of the Kennedy Krieger Institute (2012), poignantly stated: "If you've met one child with autism, well, you've met one child with autism." The basic understanding of differing student prior knowledge, motivation, and academic, emotional, social, behavioral, perceptual, developmental, physical, communicative, and sensory abilities and levels helps shape the focus of inclusion decisions. Even though students may share a disability label, they are individuals foremost. Nor are any two teachers the same. Teachers and staff possess different personalities, beliefs, informational needs, and experiences (Knight, 2009). Consequently each inclusive environment requires understandings that yield compassionate inclusive decisions that acknowledge an *inclusion spectrum.*

Differentiate

Lesson designs are specifically written to be within students' zones of proximal development (Vygotsky, 1962, 1978) to teach students on their instructional levels, minus the frustrations. Daily, weekly, monthly, quarterly, and annual plans honor research-based interventions and curriculum standards. Designs include research on the way students learn best, such as connecting the learning to something already known and educating students in stress-free environments. Lesson designs honor multiple intelligences, individual student profiles, and cooperative peer supports. Lessons are designed with objectives, procedures, and assessments that match individual and classroom dynamics. Designs outline the big ideas and ways to help students continually absorb those concepts (Wiggins & McTighe, 2006).

Evaluate

This is where the cycle goes back to the learning. Goals are outlined, instruction is given, and achievements are evaluated. Informal and formal assessments offer valuable information that is reviewed at set timelines occurring throughout each unit of study, day, week, month, quarter, and year. Figure 3.1 elaborates more about essential inclusion actions that individualize, naturalize, collaborate, learn, understand, differentiate, and evaluate practices and achievements.

Being professional collaborators means honoring more than the philosophic inclusion principles, since the pragmatic applications breathe life into each and every classroom. Consequently, inclusion is turned into a reality with intensive planning and the ongoing sharing of general and special education resources, strategies, and knowledge. Increased knowledge catapults the cognitive, affective, sensory, communicative, and physical skills of learners within inclusive classrooms. District administrators, principals, supervisors, inclusion coaches, and school leaders foster positive staff attitudes with specific measurable inclusion goals, designed to increase the performance and knowledge of educators and students. Effective inclusion results through increased knowledge, planning, and collaboration within and beyond school settings to ensure ongoing inclusion successes.

Be Compassionate

Excellent and rigorous academic courses prepare teachers to deliver the curriculum, but another course that needs to be *included* in college and university syllabi is *Inclusion Education: Compassion 101.* Inclusion rules when compassion is infused into each and every school and classroom lesson. Compassion

Figure 3.1   INCLUDE Planner

INCLUDE Planner **(individualize, naturalize, collaborate, learn, understand, differentiate, evaluate)**	

School: **Grade:**   **Class:**

Team Members:

Professional INCLUDE Goal(s):

1. We will have high expectations for all students to achieve increased academic and functional performances (e.g., English language arts, math, science, history, music, art, technology, social, behavioral, and communication skills as assessed with progress monitoring via classroom, district, standardized assessments, observation, and anecdotal records).

2. We will design instruction that scaffolds students' learning needs to provide whole-group, small-group, and individualized learning opportunities as appropriate within the general education classroom.

3. We will improve students' learning, engaging curiosity and imagination with research-based inclusion strategies and interventions with multidisciplinary approaches.

Individualize	Students' personal strengths, preferred modalities, and individual interests will be highlighted and honored.
Naturalize	The least restrictive environment of the general education classroom will be the first option of student placement, offering an inclusive education alongside age- and grade-level peers.
Collaborate	Students will work in cooperative groups as partners to solve problems, while coaches, teachers, administrators, related staff, and families collaboratively plan together to reflect on and deliver optimum educational services to all students.
Learn	Specific core curriculum standards that students need to learn, how they will learn them, and the effectiveness of the instruction will be outlined through the mapping of structured yearly, quarterly, monthly, weekly, and daily inclusive lesson planning.
Understand	There is a consistent understanding that the lesson pacing will vary depending on prior student knowledge, motivation, academic, emotional, social, behavioral, perceptual, developmental, physical, communicative, and sensory abilities.
Differentiate	Lessons will be within students' zones of proximal development, honoring research-based interventions with brain-based knowledge that acknowledges students' multiple ways of learning and individual learning profiles.
Evaluate	Data from informal and formal assessments will be reviewed throughout the school year and then evaluated quarterly to tweak and fine-tune the interventions based on student responses and performances from a variety of curriculum-based assessments and observations. Data will be accumulated in students' profiles and portfolios and regularly shared with collaborative teams of leaders and educators, and students and families. Timeline of formal evaluation dates: Initial planning date: _____ First review: _____ Second review: _____ Third review: _____ Fourth review: _____

(Continued)

Figure 3.1   (Continued)

INCLUDE Goals: Students, Teachers, Related Staff, and Families	Annual	Monthly	Weekly
Planning Members:			

Who?			
What?			
When?			
Where?			

INCLUDE Goals: Students, Teachers, Related Staff, and Families		Annual	Monthly	Weekly
How?				

Student Information:

Name:

Age:

Grade:

Strengths:

Interests:

Current Concerns and Coaching Notes:

within inclusive classrooms involves understanding that the difficulties many students display are not feigned ones. Compassion in inclusive buildings involves not sympathy or pity, but consideration of students' diverse academic, social, emotional, behavioral, perceptual, physical, sensory, and communicative levels. Compassion then yields lesson accommodations that help, but do not enable, students on an appropriate scaffolding continuum. Compassionate teachers are passionate about not only their subjects but also their students. This compassion is then transferred to caring learners within inclusion classrooms, school buildings, families, and communities. Compassion yields inclusion programs that venture beyond the realm of compliance to become quality inclusion education that values the whole child, not just the mastery of the standards. Compassionate leaders and teachers have high expectations that coach all of their students to succeed.

Be Structured

Inclusion structure requires framing the organization, management, and delivery of appropriate learning and social opportunities for all students. Consistent routines and expectations within structured schools and classrooms offer students who require more organization a dependable framework to follow. Professionals explore inclusion norms, expectations, and goals to apply the appropriate interventions to classrooms with opportunities for whole-group, small-group, and individual grouping within inclusive classrooms and schools. District and outside supports, along with research connections and collaborations with families, team members, related staff, and organizations, are crucial coaching factors. The ultimate goal is for administrators, principals, supervisors, coaches, instructional support teams, team leaders, GE and SE educators, related support staff, students, peers, and families to collaboratively plan for successful school and community outcomes. This process values mapping out specific structured timelines to achieve daily, weekly, monthly, quarterly, and annual goals that increase the performance and knowledge of educators and students. Inclusion is an ongoing and evolutionary process; it requires the systematic planning of professionals who collaboratively apply the evidence-based practices and interventions (Cook, Shepherd, Cook, & Cook, 2012). Documentation with fidelity to programs is essential. Instruction-based assessments offer concrete and realistic educator and student reflections on the effectiveness of classroom practices and interventions. Collaborative teams then review the data. Structure ultimately offers a framework to measure the data and to then adjust inclusion programs to achieve ongoing progress.

Be Aware

Awareness allows teams to appropriately anticipate students' needs, sometimes even before those needs surface. This falls under the domain of coaching in an environment that values UDL. No one frantically builds a ramp at an airport as a person in a wheelchair approaches, but that ramp is in place because the need is anticipated. If a person wants to roll a baby carriage or walk along that same incline, that is fine, since the universal design is an inclusive one. Closed captioning benefits students with hearing differences, yet students with dyslexia and English learners also use the services. Being cognizant of students' diverse levels stops the *learning alarms, instructional surprises,* and *inclusion panics.* These are replaced by preparedness that ties in with the aforementioned inclusion rules of professionalism, structure, compassion, and reflection. Awareness means that administrators, supervisors, teacher leaders, coaches, and educators are prepared with the appropriate research-based interventions and supports to assist students to achieve higher outcomes. This translates to having more common planning time with colleagues, and the appropriate resources, which may range from eReaders to seat cushions, SMART Tables, fraction tiles, high-interest/lower-level informational texts, and an array of diverse curriculum and instructional resources. Similar to a ramp, these proactive accommodations and strategies are inclined to benefit all learners. Bottom line, inclusion attitudes say, "We are aware of students' diverse needs and are prepared to provide the resources, time, and support required!"

Be Reflective

Mirror, mirror on the wall, who is the *inclusion fairest* of them all? Honest and candid professional inclusion reflections catapult learning successes. Before the instruction begins, teachers need coaching to formulate ways that they will establish and review student baseline levels to gauge program effectiveness. Instructional interventions are reviewed to determine student progress. This may refer but not be limited to a combination of reading, writing, listening, speaking, language, math, social, behavioral, perceptual, organizational, and physical domains. Administrators and coaches help teachers to determine if students' skills, levels, and knowledge are increased. By reviewing both formal and informal data, more reflective decisions are made. If levels are not increased, then perhaps it is the instruction and/or depth of the subject matter that needs to be tweaked. Reflective teachers within inclusive environments are coached to be a combination of the five basic inclusion rules. Reflective staff members are professional, aware, compassionate, structured, and willing to gaze into the mirror to think about how to improve practices.

PART II

Establishing Inclusion Coaching Baselines

4

Beginning Steps of an Inclusion Coaching Program

Before any inclusion coaching program (ICP) begins, data must be reviewed, with goals and objectives delineated. It is similar to an individualized education program (IEP), but in this case, the acronym ICP denotes an inclusion coaching program. As discussed in Part I, administrators take stock of their staff of teachers and population of students. Past practices and future goals are reviewed by coaches, administrators, and staff to establish inclusion plans. Teacher input is given via written surveys, professional development sessions, grade-level meetings, small-group conversations, and one-to-one collaborations.

Inclusion coaching offers ongoing support. The coaching begins with input at a whole-staff meeting or perhaps at grade-level team meetings. This involves all educators and staff, such as grade-level general and special education teachers, team members, occupational and behavioral interventionists, learning support providers, principals, directors, supervisors, lunch assistants, and special subject teachers. If some staff cannot attend the meetings, then written communications are prepared and shared ahead of time. Coaches then reflect on communicated and observed student and staff needs and offer input with nonjudgmental support to help the staff review current practices and formulate plans. Before a program begins, teachers and all staff must view the inclusion coaching as a nonthreatening entity. The sole purpose of the inclusion coaching is to ensure that every student and teacher experiences a multitude of successes. The following offers an inclusion coaching agenda and outline for a school year.

Inclusion Coaching Agenda

Topics 1–5 will be reviewed throughout the year:

1. Inclusion Strategies and Lesson Plan Designs

2. Classroom Collaboration: Co-Teaching Models, Working With Assistants

3. Connecting the Standards to the Students

4. Raising Literacy and Math Skills

5. Developing Professional Inclusion Communities

A. Whole Staff Professional Development

Professional development summer days for the faculty of general and special education teachers:

- Survey teacher, staff, and student needs; inclusion practices; co-teaching responsibilities; and curricular concerns for the upcoming school year
- Introduce and explain nonevaluative inclusion coaching roles and supports available
- Explore and align inclusion principles and differentiated instruction with appropriate interventions
- Collaboratively formulate lesson plans for quarterly, monthly, and weekly cross-curricular units of study
- Distribute and share resources and online references for student documentation, collaborative lesson planning, and cross-curricular connections

Staff will:

- Connect inclusion research to content areas and student population
- Address academic, social, and behavioral student levels with appropriate inclusion strategies and interventions that propagate good teaching practices for all students
- Share co-teaching/student concerns
- Explore instructional models
- Investigate effective collaborations with assistants and co-teachers
- Establish parity with roles and responsibilities to support each other and their students
- Connect the inclusion strategies to content areas, core standards, and individual/class needs
- Apply strategies to lesson plans to achieve quarterly, monthly, and weekly objectives
- Develop ongoing professional learning community (PLC) systems of inclusion, communication, organization, reflection, and documentation

Resources include teacher access to online classroom reproducibles, interactive PDFs, research studies, WebQuests, collaborative lesson plan formats, intervention plans, communication logs, professional online networking, and PLC study guides.

B. Inclusion Coaching Visits and Sessions (every 3–4 weeks)
   Inclusion strategies, interventions, collaborations, and supports
   Objectives and goals:

- Observe inclusion classrooms to offer feedback
- Collaborate at lesson planning sessions with whole staff, in grade-level teams, with co-teachers, and one-to-one as needed
- Collaborate and strategize with grade-level teachers
- Apply and refine inclusion strategies and interventions
- Infuse co-teaching models in lesson plans and inclusion classroom routines
- Debrief with co-teachers and related staff about lesson plans and interventions
- Revisit classrooms and teachers
- Formulate and recommend future inclusion and co-teaching strategies and practices for continued professional development

Staff of learners will:

- Strengthen co-teaching relationships and staff responsibilities
- Explore literacy and math strategies
- Connect and apply the inclusion strategies and interventions to students and curriculum
- Develop effective programs to increase student/family responsibilities, collaborations, and communications
- Increase disABILITY knowledge
- Investigate research-based practices and inclusion principles (e.g., universal design for learning [UDL], understanding by design [UbD], cooperative learning, visual-auditory-kinesthetic-tactile [VAKT] modalities, and multiple intelligences) to achieve optimum student results
- Continually review and monitor student data to document effectiveness of interventions and programs and to guide instructional decisions
- Solidify and tweak inclusion lesson plans with appropriate lessons for whole classes, small groups, and individual students

INCLUSION PRINCIPLES

The following 18 principles may seem like commonsense ones, but at times in everyone's haste to move forward, the basics are forgotten. These inclusion principles need to live and breathe in each school environment. Coaches can help teachers discover ways to apply these principles to individual classrooms and students.

Valuable and Applicable Things to Do in All Classrooms on a Daily Basis

1. Establish prior knowledge.

2. Preplan lessons with structured objectives that allow for inter/post planning.

3. Proceed from the simple to the complex by using discrete task analysis, which breaks up the learning into its parts.

4. Use a step-by-step approach, teaching in small bites, with much practice and repetition.

5. Reinforce abstract concepts with concrete examples, such as looking at a map while learning compass directions or walking around a neighborhood to read street signs.

6. Think about possible accommodations and modifications that might be needed, such as using a digital recorder for notes, reducing the amount of spelling words, and preparing enrichment assignments to engage more advanced learners.

7. Incorporate sensory elements—visual-auditory-kinesthetic-tactile ones—such as writing letters in salt trays; creating acute, right, and obtuse angles with chopsticks; or using two differently colored skeins of yarn to represent latitude and longitude.

8. Teach to strengths to help students compensate for weaknesses, such as hopping to math facts if a child loves to move about but hates numbers.

9. Concentrate upon individual children, not syndromes.

10. Provide opportunities for success to build self-esteem.

11. Give positives before negatives.

12. Use modeling with both teachers and peers.

13. Vary types of instruction and assessment, with multiple intelligences and cooperative learning across the curriculum.

14. Relate learning to children's lives, infusing information gained from observations, shared conversations, interest inventories, and student surveys.

15. Remember the basics, such as teaching students proper hygiene, social skills, respecting others, effectively listening, or reading directions on a worksheet, in addition to the 3 *Rs*: Reading, wRiting, and aRithmetic.

16. Establish a pleasant classroom environment that encourages students to ask questions and become actively involved in their learning.

17. Increase students' self-awareness of levels and progress.

18. Effectively communicate and collaborate with families, students, and colleagues, while smiling; it's contagious ☺ ☺ ☺ ☺ ☺.

Source: Adapted from Karten, T. (2010c). *Inclusion strategies that work! Research-based methods for the classroom* (2nd ed.). Thousand Oaks, CA: Corwin.

Figure 4.1 is offered as an applicable standards-based curriculum example of Inclusion Principle 7, showing a way to incorporate sensory elements with a visual element. Before students solve equations, a visual representation that depicts the difference between the power of 2 and the power of 5 is appreciated.

Figure 4.1   Inclusion Principle 7: Applicable Standards-Based Curriculum
Example

Visual Math Standard Connection:

Expressions and Equations: 6.EE.1 Write and evaluate numerical expressions involving whole number exponents.

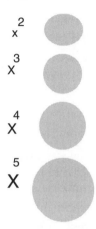

Visual dictionaries offer students many opportunities to *see* the learning! Share these sites and programs with educators:

- http://visual.merriam-webster.com

- http://www.visuwords.com

- http://www.inspiration.com

- http://www.inspiration.com/Kidspiration

Figure 4.2 is offered as an applicable curriculum example of Inclusion Principle 5, showing a way to incorporate a concrete example of an abstract concept.

Figure 4.2 Inclusion Principle 5: Applicable Standards-Based Curriculum Example

English Language Arts Standards in Science and Technical Subjects in Grades 9–10, RST.9–10.5:

Analyze the structure of the relationships among concepts in a text, including relationships among key terms (e.g., force, friction, reaction force, energy).
Students pantomime:

- Skating on a grassy surface versus skating on a concrete surface
- Pushing a shopping cart
- Pulling a wagon
- Newton's three laws of motion
- Difference between potential and kinetic energy
- Baseball players sliding onto a base

Figure 4.3 is offered as an example of Inclusion Principle 14, relating to students' lives and shared connections with a kindergarten-level core standard in reading informational text.

Figure 4.3 Inclusion Principle 14: Applicable Standards-Based Curriculum Example

RI.K.3. With prompting and support, describe the connection between two individuals, events, ideas, or pieces of information in a text.

Motivate a kindergartner to pick a choice-generated text based on his or her favorite topics, before introducing how to research informational skills. Then ask students to pair together in small groups to share learning on topics ranging from giant pandas to Ruby Bridges.

Figure 4.4 is offered as an applicable example of Inclusion Principle 17, showing a way for students to increase their self-awareness of levels and progress.

Figure 4.4 Inclusion Principle 17: Applicable Standards-Based Curriculum Example

Name: _____ Date: _____

Thinking About Learning

Directions: Rate the difficulty level of an assignment. Be honest with yourself as you evaluate your understanding of the topic. If you find that you are not sure or are very confused about a topic, ask a teacher, peer, or teacher's assistant for help. This will keep you on the right track!

Name: _____ Date: _____

Subject: _____

Topic: _____

Text Pages and/or Assignment: _____

Circle the rating: E, M or T.

    E = Easy "I understand this!"

    M = Medium "I'm not sure about this topic."

    T = Tough "Hard to understand."

My comments: _____

_____

_____

_____

_____

Source: Karten, T. (2008b). *Inclusion activities that work! Grades 6–8.* Thousand Oaks, CA: Corwin.

Invite educators to note (in a form such as Figure 4.5) how they are applying these 18 principles to benefit their learners across populations, subject areas, and grade levels.

Figure 4.5 How I/We Will Infuse These Big Ideas into Lessons

1. Establishing prior knowledge	
2. Thinking about pre-inter-post planning	
3. Applying discrete task analysis	
4. Offering practice and repetition	
5. Showing concrete examples	
6. Providing accommodations and modifications for all students	
7. Using visual-auditory-kinesthetic-tactile sensory elements	
8. Teaching to student strengths	
9. Concentrating on children, not syndromes	
10. Increasing self-esteem	
11. Offering positives before negatives	
12. Modeling	
13. Varying instruction and assessments with multiple intelligences and cooperative learning	
14. Relating to students' lives	
15. Teaching basics and 3 *R*s across curricula	
16. Setting up a pleasant class atmosphere with active learning	
17. Increasing student self-awareness	
18. Communicating and collaborating	

EMBRACING INCLUSION NORMS, EXPECTATIONS, AND RESOURCES

Developing norms and expectations include inquiry, reflection, planning, and application to achieve ongoing improvements. Each individual who is part of the collaborative team needs to wholeheartedly believe in student successes. This acronymic sentence summarizes the elements: *I promise each child will succeed.*

I nclusion norms

P lanning and preparation

E volution

C ollaboration and communication

W illingness

S caffolding, supports, and strategies

Inclusion Norms

I, as the first letter, advocates that inclusion programs start with the establishment of norms and expectations that collaborative inclusion communities create at the onset of the year. The open-ended sentences in Figure 4.6 are intended to invite additional norms and expectations. Read on for further insights into how to ensure that staff fulfill the promise that each child will succeed. The open spaces invite collaborative teams to offer their insights.

Figure 4.6 Inclusion Norms: Establishment and Expectations

Inclusion Norms

Students will become self-regulated learners.

Students will

Teachers will respect the students, each other, support staff, and their curriculum.

Teachers will

Families will collaborate and communicate with teachers.

Families will

Administrators, supervisors, staff developers, and coaches will listen to and support teachers' concerns.

Administrators, supervisors, staff developers, and coaches will

---

Planning and Preparation

Today's diverse classrooms demand that educators have a high degree of preparedness if students are to master the curriculum standards. Staff development plans need to focus on setting up applicable inclusion programs. This includes offering teachers the structure and support to help students achieve the learning goals (Killion, 2008).

Grant Wiggins and Jay McTighe (2006) emphasize mapping the big ideas before instruction or assessments are given. Figure 4.7 emphasizes the basics of inclusion planning and preparation.

Figure 4.7   Big Ideas of Inclusion

What are the Big Ideas we want to achieve in our inclusion coaching programs?	/Outcomes
• Hmm . . . how will we achieve these goals?	/Procedures
• How will we determine the success of the inclusion programs?	/Assessments
• Hmm . . . what will we do next?	/Follow-ups
The Big Ideas of our inclusion programs:	
This is how we will achieve these goals:	
Our program assessments will include:	
Future inclusion plans include:	
Inclusion teachers can fill in these Big Ideas to individual classrooms:	
• What are the Big Ideas we want students to know?	/Outcomes
• Hmm . . . how can we teach the lesson/unit?	/Procedures
• How will we determine if the concepts are learned?	/Assessments
• Hmm . . . what will we do next?	/Follow-ups
The Big Ideas that we want students to know:	
This is how we will teach this lesson/unit:	
Our assessments will include:	
Future lessons will:	

Evolutionary

Inclusion is not a program, but a process—like creating art, cooking a meal, learning to sound out words, solving a long division problem, or investigating a scientific hypothesis. It requires that staff map out annual, quarterly, monthly, weekly, and daily objectives. This will be delineated later on with specific curriculum examples.

Collaboration and Communication

Without these skills, we revert back to a time when teachers closed their doors and taught in isolation, without administrators, co-teachers, inclusion teams, and families working side by side. Inclusion strength lies in the combination of interactions and the collaborative skills of many professionals, not on the shoulders of individual administrators, educators, related staff, students, peers, or families.

Willingness

I often bring rulers, rubber bands, and sponges to professional development sessions to concretely demonstrate the following concepts. Rulers measure progress, rubber bands are intended to represent flexibility, and sponges represent the absorption of concepts. Hence, professionals determine student levels, yet they also figure out innovative ways for students to gain or *soak up* skills. Willingness refers to flexible attitudes within structured programs that advocate inclusive learning opportunities for all students and staff.

Scaffolding, Supports, and Strategies

The classroom strategies and interventions are not uniform ones. Each student has differing academic, communicative, emotional, social, behavioral, perceptual, physical, and developmental levels, skills, and motivations. Consequently, the scaffolding, supports, and strategies will be diverse ones as well. If the general education classroom is determined to be the appropriate placement for a student, then the scaffolding and the supplementary services provided by the staff provide appropriate accommodations that support, but do not enable, students.

When each professional says, "I promise each child will succeed," each and every student and staff member is an inclusive winner!

5

Adaptations, Skills, and Differentiation

APPROPRIATE ACCOMMODATIONS

There is a difference between accommodations and modifications as denoted in the following researchers' definitions in reference to assessments.

"*Accommodations* are defined as changes to test content, format, or administration conditions for particular test takers that do not change the construct being measured but do remove construct-irrelevant contributions to test scores that would otherwise exist for these individuals. *Modifications* are defined as changes in test content, format, and/or administration conditions that are made to increase accessibility for some individuals but that affect the construct measured and, consequently, result in scores that differ in meaning from scores from the unmodified assessment" (Warren et al., 2011, p. 4).

This concept of accommodations and modifications is not exclusive to students but is applicable to all parties who are involved in the inclusion implementation. Administrators, supervisors, educators, and students are all at different levels of proficiency and require different levels of support. The inclusion knowledge, skills, experiences, and attitudes of individuals within each group vary from people who are experts or veterans in the field to those who are less experienced or novices. Some individuals will be more receptive to collaboration, while others prefer to go solo. Regardless of people's levels, building administrators, team leaders, and coaches continually communicate that stagnation is never an option. Sharing ideas in a nonthreatening format at meetings while accommodating or modifying formats and agendas to apply to individual educators' levels is crucial. Listening and respecting each other is a two-way street.

With family input, accommodations and modifications are delineated in students' IEPs; however, they also need to be reviewed throughout the year. Together, teachers and coaches decide if the accommodations and/or modifications are appropriate ones or need to be revised. If modifications are given, then those modifications are reviewed throughout the year to see if students are gaining enough skills to consider fading support. The same holds true with accommodations, since students need to learn how to accomplish more skills on their own. In addition, technology offers students built-in accommodations with assessments, but similar accommodations need to be reflected during instructional times to ensure that the assessments accurately reflect the learning experiences. Accommodations with differentiated instruction range from preparing materials in Braille, using assistive listening devices, using iPads, and reading directions aloud to providing cognitive organizers, scribes, extra time, and more. Each decision requires an examination of each student's needs. The goal is to accommodate the student but not enable him or her to the point that learned helplessness or overreliance on service providers, family members, or peers is created.

Together, teachers, instructional coaches, team members, families, and students review and reflect on the accommodations to ensure that they lead students to a road of independence. The best scenario is to provide all students with access to the accommodations with approaches that value UDL principles. For instance, encourage teachers to stock a classroom strategy table with colored overlays, reading trackers, differently sized pencils, pencil grips, electronic spellers, sheet blockers, page magnifiers, vocabulary flashcards, earphones, calculators, graph paper, counters, rulers, protractors, and more. Accommodations help learners gather, categorize, and organize as well as remain challenged through a variety of engaging instructional presentations and resources to become self-regulated learners. *Different* does not mean *incapable*. For example, if a student cannot communicate verbally, then providing access to augmentative and alternative communication programs is an appropriate accommodation to help the student express himself or herself through pictures and symbols. Educators also benefit from accommodations and supports, ranging from applicable professional development to access to appropriate learning resources and extra planning time.

Structured lesson plans offer educators guided road maps to ensure that good teaching practices accompany accommodations or modifications with careful implementation and monitoring. Every student with a disability in an inclusive classroom requires individual attention. Prescriptive accommodations and modifications offer students challenges minus the frustrations or learning situations that disseminate too much help. Coaches assist educators to maximize learning opportunities for students on all levels without sacrificing the curriculum or offering the educators too much help. Reflections yield decisions on appropriate accommodations for instruction and assessments. Figure 5.1 offers ideas for weekly class interventions and curriculum-based assessments for students. Please note that although accommodations and modifications are prescriptive ones, high expectations are not optional for any student or educator.

INCLUSION PRACTICES

Inclusion and baseball have a few things in common. Inclusion, a three-syllable multifaceted concept, has defined baselines with scores of players. Both

Figure 5.1 Class Monitoring and Curriculum-Based Assessments and Weekly Interventions

Inclusion Strategies

Weekly Class Interventions

- □ alternate materials
- □ assignments modified
- □ assistive technology
- □ assistive cues and options
- □ behavior interventions
- □ classwide peer tutoring/ mentoring
- □ collaborative projects
- □ concrete presentations
- □ cooperative learning groups
- □ co-teaching
  - □ bouncing ideas
  - □ parallel teaching
  - □ one lead, one assist
  - □ small groups/1:1
  - □ stations/centers
  - □ team/staff consultation/services
- □ debates
- □ differentiation of objectives
- □ discussion
- □ empowerment of students
- □ enrichment activities
- □ family involvement
- □ graphic organizers
- □ guided practice
- ☑ high expectations
- □ interdisciplinary lessons
- □ intervention/data groups
- □ literature circles
- □ modeling
- □ multiple intelligences
  - □ bodily and kinesthetic
  - □ existentialist
  - □ interpersonal
  - □ intrapersonal
  - □ logical- mathematical
  - □ musical-rhythmic
  - □ naturalistic
  - □ verbal-linguistic
  - □ visual-spatial
- □ note taking modified
- □ praise increased
- □ pre-teaching/prior knowledge
- □ private signals
- □ repetition/ re-teaching
- □ role playing
- □ scaffolding/step-by- step
- □ seating/teacher proximity
- □ simulations
- □ sponge activities
- □ study skill support
- □ tactile activities and materials
- □ thematic lessons
- □ time extended for responses
- □ UbD
- □ UDL
- □ visuals/more graphics
- □ writing reduced

Class Monitoring and Curriculum-Based Assessments

- □ advance notice for quizzes or tests
- □ alternate assessments
- □ attention/behavior checks
- □ baseline level established
- □ benchmarks given
- □ chapter test
- □ collaborative assignments
- □ efforts monitored
- □ exit cards
- □ extra credit/bonus questions offered
- □ FBAs-functional behavioral assessments
- □ grading and/or HW modified
- □ homework graded
- □ individual assignments/ learning contracts
- □ informal checks
- □ journals and logs checked
- □ KWL charts
- □ long-term projects
- □ multiple intelligences
  - □ bodily kinesthetic
- □ existentialist
- □ interpersonal
- □ intrapersonal
- □ logical- mathematical
- □ musical-rhythmic
- □ verbal-linguistic
- □ naturalistic
- □ verbal-spatial
- □ multiple test formats and deliveries
- □ answers recorded
- □ clutter reduced
- □ fewer/simplified concepts
- □ less/other choices
- □ less questions
- □ questions read
- □ quieter setting
- □ verbal responses
- □ vocabulary simplified/explained
- □ notebook checks
- □ observations
- □ open-books tests
- □ participation graded
- □ portfolios
- □ posttests given
- □ pretests given
- □ progress recorded
- □ re-test offered/ points for corrections
- □ rubrics distributed
- □ self-assessments
- □ self-regulation/ learning journals
- □ student conferencing
- □ study guides
- □ quizzes
- □ take-home test
- □ time extended/ pacing varied
- □ unit test
- □ UbD
- □ weekly test
- □ work lesson samples

Other Interventions:

Other Monitoring and Assessments:

Source: Karten, T. (2011). *Inclusion lesson plan book for the 21st century* (Teacher training edition). Port Chester, NY: Dude Publishing. Used with permission.

inclusion and baseball generate teams of players who follow managerial and administrative directives. Of course, there are differences between the educational service and the athletic game. This is especially noted when the attendance and finances generated at a baseball stadium infinitely supersede the number of students and monetary supports in an inclusion classroom. However, when inclusion and baseball are compared, the concept of inclusion becomes a bit less intimidating to someone who may be *a new player up at bat.*

Let us first investigate the role of a coach, one who requires that his or her players have a game plan with specific strategies and skills to learn, working with individuals and as a team. No one would expect a rookie to hit a ball out of the park without the proper training, equipment, and supports. Practice drills, work-outs, books, videos, and professional coaching sessions improve strength, skill, and endurance. Rookies then evolve into seasoned all-stars who play in fields across stadiums and countries with set schedules and resources allocated. Professional players who land on bases are applauded, but they also depend upon their teammates to advance to the next base. In addition, players who hit one *out of the park* must always step on one base at a time, before running to home plate to score a run. Pitchers throw curve balls, sliders, fastballs, and changeups. Hitters need to be ready for each pitch, no matter what the speed or whether it is within their strike zone. Baseball, a challenging sport, involves much more than holding a ticket to enter the stadium; it includes coaches who prepare, encourage, support, teach, and appreciate their players as part of a professional team.

Hence, inclusion is like a game of baseball. Sheer physical presence of students in the inclusion classroom does not ensure success. Educators working together are the professionals who coach students to evolve into proficient learners, one step or base at a time with a variety of strategies, interventions, and ongoing collaborations. Singles, doubles, triples, and home runs incrementally happen when teachers carefully structure learning objectives that match students' proficiencies. Baseball coaches and managers review the stats, while educators, team members, inclusion coaches, professional learning communities, curriculum supervisors, and principals review the assessments to ascertain students' strengths and weaknesses to guide instructional choices. Baseline levels offer vital information about which students need direct skill instruction, practice, remediation, and/or enrichment. Students are part of a class, acting as individual learners, cooperative learning teams, and consummate peer collaborators. Coaching fosters a great team spirit (Allison & Harbour, 2009). Planning for inclusion successes requires allocating the time, resources, physical setups, and ongoing support to develop and sustain productive collegial relationships. Every classroom game plan is unique, but each person is encouraged to continually exhibit a winning attitude. When inclusion is implemented in that *classroom playing field,* professionals root for and collaborate with each and every player!

It is essential to understand the type of supports teachers require. The survey in Figure 5.2 offers team leaders, administrative personnel, and inclusion coaches vital input for planning coaching sessions and support needed. It can be filled out independently and/or collaboratively. Structuring the inclusion program is an essential first step. A survey such as Figure 5.2 might be given to staff before coaching sessions begin to determine current inclusion and co-teaching levels, experiences, and concerns. This valuable feedback then structures the coaching and professional development sessions that follow.

Figure 5.2 Inclusion Survey

Teacher: _____ School: _____ Date: _____

Please circle the descriptor of your primary responsibilities:

Gen. ed. teacher   Spec. ed. teacher   Inclusion support teacher   Administrator

Related staff   Other: _____

Grade(s): _____ Subject(s): _____

E-mail: _____ Other contact info: _____

Prep times or best times to meet:

M _____ T _____ W _____ Th _____ F _____

Dates: _____

These two pages share a brief snapshot to help formulate productive inclusion coaching sessions. Thanks for your candid and valuable inclusion input.*

	1 Strongly Agree	2 Agree	3 Somewhat Agree	4 Disagree	5 Strongly Disagree
1. I have the necessary training to successfully implement inclusion.					
2. Inclusion is working well in my classroom(s) this year (if applicable).					
3. Inclusion offers academic benefits for students with disabilities.					
4. Inclusion offers social/emotional benefits for students with disabilities.					
5. Inclusion offers benefits for students without disabilities.					
6. It is difficult to modify instruction and teaching style to address the needs of some students with disabilities.					
7. I have the necessary resources to successfully implement inclusion.					
8. I have the support from other teachers, staff, and administration.					
9. I have enough time and various ways to communicate and collaborate with others.					
10. I need more information about certain disabilities.					

*Use this space to elaborate on any of the above responses or to add information on a specific inclusion class or student(s).

(Continued)

Figure 5.2 (Continued)

Top 5 List: Choose five of the following inclusion topics, placing a 1 by the area for which you would most like inclusion coaching, support, and/or information and a 5 to indicate a lesser ranking.

Lesson design for whole class, small groups, and individual learners	
Inclusion strategies	
Student accommodations	
Knowledge about disabilities/inclusion	
Effective co-teaching/collaboration practices	
Communication with families	
Assessments and data application	
Classroom management	
Cooperative learning	
Behavioral plans	
Research/resources	
Professional networking	
Reading comprehension strategies	
Word decoding skills	
Math interventions	
Writing skills	
Other content/skill area (please specify):	
Study skills	
Interdisciplinary lessons	
Peer supports/sensitivities	
Technology options	
Other area of need (please specify):	

LEARNER PROFILES

Improving students' skills and sharpening their acumen require that teachers possess a high degree of preparedness. The challenges of inclusion are acknowledged by the fact that each student within the same grade or class possesses varying prior knowledge, experiences, motivation, and family supports with unique learner profiles. However, when educators capitalize on the strengths of their students, significant rewards are yielded (Karten, 2007, 2010b; Reeves, 2011). The first step is to admit that inclusion has no standard definition, but it is an elastic concept that at times requires both flexible and structured programs, depending on individual educator and student profiles, classroom dynamics, district mandates, community and family involvements, and of course legislative directives. Therefore, inclusion has a huge color scale with various hues and tones that continually unfold. Inclusion masterpieces are consequently created and not mass-produced. Steady inclusion momentum means that even though challenges are presented, the strengths of all inclusion participants help students achieve mastery. Accommodations must ultimately provide both challenges and support (Algozzine, Daunic, & Smith, 2010) with respectful and reflective assessments (Salend, 2009). The rudimentary learner profile in Figure 5.3 depicts the importance of identifying the strengths of each student to determine a professional action plan. Team leaders, coaches, and educators complete these collaboratively (see Figure 5.4).

LESSON DIFFERENTIATION

Administrators often enter inclusive classrooms wanting to see lesson differentiation. However, there is sometimes a communication gap with *differentiating opinions* about what constitutes quality differentiation. Differentiation is applicable across the grade levels for curriculum and skills. Differentiation of instruction does not occur automatically unless educators are offered insights on what it looks like in their individual classrooms. This involves an approach that empowers both educators and students with multiple ways to teach and learn. It involves preassessments, flexible grouping, scaffolding, compacting, and both formative and summative evaluations. Terms such as *compacting*, or assessing and documenting what the students already know and do not know, offers meaningful student engagement that is based on the students' prior knowledge (Tomlinson, 1999). Inclusion coaches help educators apply these differentiated approaches in subjects across the curriculum.

Sometimes coaches also need to compact professional development for teachers since many teachers know the basic philosophy of inclusion but now want more practical strategies to connect inclusion with their curriculum and students. What is taught and how it is taught and assessed are viable ongoing inclusion conversations that determine what that inclusive classroom looks like on a daily basis with options for educators to work with the whole class, work in small groups, and provide one-on-one instruction. Aligning and

Figure 5.3 Learner Profile: Example

Student Name, Date of Birth, and Grade	Strengths (VAKT) and Multiple Intelligences	Interests: School/ Outside	Objectives: Academic, Social/Emotional, Behavioral, Physical, and Communication	Inclusion Action Plan, Accommodations, Modifications, and Recommendations	Timeline to Review Results
Larry Mist Learn 12/8/06 Third grade	Above grade-level word decoding Good visual-spatial and intrapersonal skills Excellent oral expression with adults	Art Computers Pets World history	LML will: • Increase eye contact in conversations with peers and adults • Improve inferential reading comprehension skills • Self-monitor time on academic tasks in school and at home • Solve one-step grade-level math problems involving addition and/ or subtraction	• Identify current comprehension level with informal reading assessment • Capitalize on LML's interests and strengths • Offer reading passages with global issues, historical fiction, and graphic novels • Create and integrate math word problems with dogs, cats, hamsters, and other pets • Incorporate charted and graphed behavioral plan to increase cooperative learning and time on task • Teacher conference with LML • Computer programs for reading and math skills (e.g., Funbrain.com, BrainPOP, Wordle, AutoSummarize) • Use graphic organizers and provide more visuals • Journaling • Motivate with art	• Weekly portfolio review of completed math and reading assignments • Daily review and weekly graphing of behavioral intervention plan • Weekly communication log with family to monitor/share time on task in class and for homework completion • Administer informal reading assessment • Quarterly grades

68

Figure 5.4   Learner Profile: Professional Activity

Professional activity: Collaboratively complete this learner profile for a student.

Learner Profile					
Student Name, Date of Birth, and Grade	*Strengths (VAKT) and Multiple Intelligences*	*Interests: School/ Outside*	*Objectives: Academic Social/Emotional, Behavioral, Physical, and Communication*	*Inclusion Action Plan, Accommodations, Modifications, and Recommendations*	*Timeline to Review Results*

differentiating the tasks, objectives, processes, content, and assessments to maximize educator and hence student abilities and levels are crucial. Coaches help staff think about different levels of instruction and the possible accommodations required.

The next rubric, Figure 5.5, is intended as a tool that administrators, leaders, and coaches share with educators to outline the categories and degrees of differentiation.

Figure 5.5a Differentiation Rubric

Domains	4	3	2	1
Instructional Objectives and Activities	Lesson unit of study includes differentiation of instructional objectives and activities for all levels of learners (e.g., baseline, more advanced, and challenging objectives)	Lesson unit of study includes differentiation of objectives and activities for a majority of learners in the class	Lesson unit of study includes differentiated objectives and activities for a single learner or small group	Lesson unit of study includes same objectives and activities for whole class with one level of learning and instruction present
Prior Knowledge	Establishes all students' prior knowledge before formal instruction	Establishes prior knowledge for most of the class before formal instruction	Establishes prior knowledge for a few learners before formal instruction	No evidence or establishment of students' prior knowledge before formal instruction
Motivation and Connections	Clearly succeeds in tapping students' strengths and interests with motivating and meaningful lesson connections and products that develop student metacognition and pride of learning	Attempts to tap into students' strengths and interests with motivating and meaningful connections and products that acknowledge student metacognition	Taps into a few of the students' strengths and interests with sporadic student connections in lessons, but no metacognition is established	Clearly ignores student strengths and interests; no attempt or evidence of motivating and meaningful student connections or metacognition present
Grouping	Appropriate consideration given to whole class, small group, and 1:1 instruction at all lesson stages	Consideration of whole class, small group, and 1:1 instruction at some lesson stages	Minor consideration of whole class, small group, and 1:1 instruction during lesson	Consideration of whole class, small group, and 1:1 instruction not present
Instructional Strategies and Assessments	Consistent evidence of a multitude of instructional strategies with formal and/or informal assessments with the infusion of three or more of the following: heterogeneous cooperative learning groups, multiple intelligences, VAKT elements, and technology	Some variation of both instruction and assessments with at least two of the following: heterogeneous cooperative learning groups, multiple intelligences, VAKT elements, and technology	Differentiation of only one domain: either instruction or assessment with one of the following: cooperative learning, multiple intelligences, VAKT elements, and technology	Lack of evidence of differentiation of instruction and assessments; no demonstration of cooperative learning, multiple intelligences, VAKT elements, or technology present in lesson planning
Scaffolding	Consistent appropriate scaffolding with accommodations and modifications in lessons that help but do not enable students	Some offering of accommodations and modifications in lessons, but usually the same scaffolding for most students	Inappropriate accommodations, modifications, and/or scaffolding in lessons (e.g., too much or too little)	All students learn the same way without including accommodations, modifications, or scaffolding in lessons
Enrichment and Remediation	Multitude of opportunities for enrichment and remediation (e.g., ongoing stations and centers)	Some opportunities for enrichment and remediation	Sporadic opportunities for either enrichment or remediation	No opportunities for either enrichment or remediation

Figure 5.5b   Differentiation Ideas

Subject: Unit: Concepts: Differentiated Lesson Unit	
Domains	Educators collaboratively differentiate the learning for a unit of study.
Instructional Objectives and Standards	Baseline Knowledge: Advancing Level: More Challenging Assignments:
Motivation and Connections	
Student Activities	Cubing, tic-tac-toe boards, anchor and sponge activities, learning contracts, compacting, cooperative groups, independent practice, centers
Co-Teaching Models	Staff and assistants bouncing ideas off each other, parallel teaching, one leading/one assisting, small groups/1:1, stations/centers, consultation
Grouping: Whole Class, Small Group, and 1:1	Set up an ongoing structured system of groups within the classroom (instead of pullout). Recommend 10–12 min. twice a week for review, on-level, and challenging assignments with smaller groups of students—sending a strong communication for students to be prepared and not wait for the day before the test to ask questions and gain clarifications. This circumvents misconceptions from escalating. This ongoing classroom setup communicates the importance of review for *all* students, and offers the students with IEPs more in-class support without singling them out and allows more advanced students to continue their learning on higher levels.
Instructional Strategies and Assessments	
Scaffolding and Accommodations	
Enrichment and Remediation	
Follow-Up/Revisitation Plans	
Other ideas and comments:	

6

Curriculum Planning

"Planning is bringing the future into the present so you can do something about it now" (ThinkExist, 2012a). As mentioned before, the principles of understanding by design (UbD), a curricular model developed by Grant Wiggins and Jay McTighe (2006), employs a backward design that has the goals and assessments outlined before learning activities are developed. To illustrate this point, aside from nomadic tribes, most people prepare travel itineraries rather than arbitrarily ending up somewhere. Detailed arrangements do not proceed until travelers figure out where they'd like to visit. The same planning holds true for education models that require teachers to have structured learning destinations before they plan their lessons. This involves looking at the school year's "big picture" with respective yearly, then quarterly, monthly, weekly, and daily plans (see Figure 6.1).

Figure 6.1 Curriculum Goals at a Glance

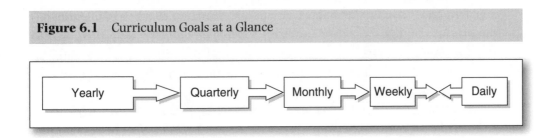

Daily lesson plans often intertwine with the weekly ones. Daily and weekly demands outside the curriculum—from assemblies to evacuation drills, nurse visits, conferences, and more—often interfere with intended lesson plans. Quite often what teachers perceive to be a 5-minute lesson ends up taking 55 minutes, while sometimes those 55-minute lessons occur within 5 minutes.

Hence one day might require enrichment for some students, while other students require repetition to achieve mastery. Seeing the big picture for each quarter and month helps each week and day to be realistically planned. Educators may perceive mapping out the year at the onset as a daunting task, but teachers need to be coached to view the merits of this type of planning. The rest of the year becomes smooth sailing in terms of pacing when goals and learning outcomes are clearly delineated. Teachers do not write detailed plans; they just write rough drafts in terms of what they would like to accomplish during set quarters of the year and each month. Then those plans are translated into weekly/daily lessons. Inserting the Common Core State Standards into this model is a way to accomplish this task, along with reviewing the content in teachers' manuals and texts. Like social studies textbooks that offer historical events depicted in timelines, inclusive classrooms emulate this design for their yearly course of study. Mapping principles are applied to elementary, middle school, and high school subjects as shown in Figures 6.2–6.4. Offering educators the time to design these collaborative planners at the beginning of the year (see Figure 6.5) and opportunities to revisit them at set collaborative professional development meetings is time well spent. These next charts offer curriculum examples of quarterly and monthly plans for reading and language arts (Figure 6.2), algebra (Figure 6.3), and physics (6.4).

ACCESS TO THE GENERAL EDUCATION CURRICULUM

As delineated in the Individuals with Disabilities Education Act (IDEA) of 1997, IEP goals are connected to the curriculum of the general education class. Coaches need to reinforce that an IEP is not a substitute for the curriculum, since students need exposure to the more intricate complexities of the general education curriculum to become successful independent thinkers. When students possess motor, sensory, information processing, social, emotional, or behavioral differences, then the instructional methods and materials sometimes differ, but deleting curriculum standards is nonnegotiable. This may require an accommodation or a modification ranging from using pencil grips to sign language, large print books, study guides, mnemonics, peer mediation, differently leveled text, learning contracts, or maybe teaching a student how to use the AutoSummarize tool. Access to general education means setting up high standards for all students to learn and taking the appropriate steps to ensure that happens.

The IRIS Center (n.d.) has interactive teacher modules titled *Accessing the General Education Curriculum: Inclusion Considerations for Students With Disabilities.* These modules speak about a continuum of services that offer curriculum that is aligned with the standards. Having an attitude that students cannot learn something because it is too complex is not an option. Principals need to review the data on large-scale assessments. The results have to be looked at over multiple years and in multiple ways to track the effectiveness of programs for students with disabilities. The next step engages collaborative

Figure 6.2 Quarterly Lesson Plan Units for Reading and Language Arts (Second Grade)

First-Quarter Goals and Objectives

Reading Comprehension: To identify story elements (characters, setting, plot, climax, resolution)
To identify reality versus fantasy
To strengthen comprehension and critical thinking skills with main idea, sequencing, and cause-effect
To use context clues to identify unfamiliar vocabulary words

Language Arts: To express and expand written thoughts in well-constructed sentences with interest-generated informational stories and in response to reading passages

- To recognize and develop proper sentence structure with daily language drills
- To recognize parts of speech to apply capitalization and punctuation rules
- To develop the writing process

Introduction to homonyms, synonyms, and antonyms
A–Z lists, writing frames, and webs

Word decoding/encoding:
To strengthen word attack skills
To apply phonetic patterns to weekly spelling words
Review of closed syllables and short vowel sounds in multisyllabic words
Digraphs: *ch, sh, wh, th*
Open syllables in two-syllable words
Final *e* syllable, *r*-controlled vowels
Irregular plurals

Study Skills: To organize work in assignment pads and calendars for short-range and long-term assignments

Technology: To properly use the mouse and keyboard to access programs

Perceptual: To attend to teachers and peers, filtering out distracting stimuli
To strengthen visual tracking skills

Social/Behavior: To follow all classroom and school rules with academics and behavior (e.g., homework, attention, time on task, transitions)

Second-Quarter Goals and Objectives

Reading Comprehension: To work cooperatively in literature circles as artists, passage pickers, word wizards, and connectors across selected fiction and nonfiction texts
To strengthen comprehension and critical thinking skills with supporting details and drawing conclusions
To continue to read various types of literature
To enhance online and hands-on dictionary skills to identify unfamiliar vocabulary

(Continued)

75

Figure 6.2 (Continued)

Language Arts: To improve writing with descriptive vocabulary-sensory elements, transitional words, and expanders in one to two paragraphs, personal narratives, and reports Daily language drills for capitalization and punctuation Introduction to words with multiple meanings and dictionary skills Morphology charts To identify word parts (structural analysis) To strengthen skills with antonyms, synonyms, homophones, and multiple meaning words To utilize organization and proofreading skills To develop more sophisticated word choices
Word decoding/encoding: To strengthen word attack skills Vowel teams: *ai, ay; eigh, oa; oe, ow; ee, ea; ey, ie* Review contractions, diphthongs: *oi, oy, ou, ow, au, aw, oo, ue, ew* Prefixes: *re-, un-, dis-* Suffixes: *-es, -ed, -ing, -er, est, -less*, doubling rule Review syllabication skills with words in stories read To apply phonetic patterns to weekly spelling words
Study Skills: To learn how to extract information from science and social studies texts using headings as guides with modeling and oral and written questions
Technology: To explore keyboard skills with Word documents, implementing language and spelling tools
Perceptual: To develop listening skills by identifying the main idea and drawing conclusions from orally read stories Continue with visual tracking skills
Social/Behavior: To assist peers with assigned cooperative roles in stations and centers; follow all established class rules
Third-Quarter Goals and Objectives
Reading Comprehension: To understand the motives of characters and the sequencing of events and to analyze information presented in grade-level texts and fiction genres
Language Arts: To proofread writings in descriptive essays, using rubrics, samples, and input from peer and teacher conferences Daily language drills for capitalization and punctuation To strengthen creative writing skills To introduce poetry unit with diamantes
Word decoding/encoding: To introduce and strengthen: Schwa sound /u/, -c/e syllable Suffixes: *-ness, -ful, -ly, -able* Hard sounds of *c* and *g*

Social/Behavior: To increase self-awareness by tallying on-task behavior

Study Skills: To strengthen metacognitive skills as self-regulated learners, recording and graphing progress in reading and other content areas

Technology: To work collaboratively with educational software

Perceptual: Listening skills with unfamiliar words
Timed visual tracking

Fourth-Quarter Goals and Objectives

Reading Comprehension: To accurately and independently answer oral and written inferential questions in fiction and nonfiction genres with teacher and student-chosen texts

Language Arts: To apply figurative language in writings and to publish selected works from writing journals
To publish short picture books
To apply varying sentence structure
To continue developing proofreading skills
To write limericks

Word decoding/encoding:
Spelling pattern: -igh, k spelled c, k, ck, ic
Review of all syllable types
Oral and written dictations
Apply skills with all vocabulary

Social/Behavior: To exhibit social reciprocity in all classroom activities and school interactions with peers and adults

Study Skills: To monitor progress in all content areas by reviewing graphed grades in portfolios

Technology: To create PowerPoint presentations on reading, math, science, and social studies units learned

Perceptual: Strengthen eye-hand coordination to follow oral and written directions, while filtering out distractions

Instructional Materials: Project Read—Phonology, Framing Your Thoughts, report form, short novels, second grade–level texts, phonics workbooks, Wilson Reading System—Levels 1–6, Spectrum Reading—Grade 2, understanding context clues, drawing conclusions, Listening Skills Kit, Daily Language Review—Grade 2, computer PowerPoints, online dictionaries and computer tools, Reading A–Z, BrainPOP, Kidspiration, Toon University, Funbrain.com, Edhelper.com, Cues & Comprehension, phonics dictionaries, teacher-made worksheets, spelling notebooks, writing journals, *Scholastic News*, online articles, creative writing folders, poetry units
Assessments: Weekly reading comprehension, phonics, language arts, spelling quizzes, writing portfolios, listening, perceptual and study skill progress graphed, teacher observation and student recording of behavior. Book reports, cloze exercises, quarterly developmental reading assessments, word identification, and phonics inventories

Source: Adapted from Karten, T. (2011). *Inclusion lesson plan book for the 21st century* (Teacher training edition). Port Chester, NY: Dude Publishing.

Fifth-Grade Long-Range Monthly Plans

August	Review IEPs and 504s [or Section 504 accommodation plans] with teams and share accommodations with all staff, multiple intelligences, class survey, school rules, Mathematics Dynamic Assessment to assess math facts, interests, problem-solving levels, developmental reading assessments to establish word identification levels, fluency, and reading comprehension, home communication logs, summer sharing, Back-to-School night, class jobs and rules established
September	Map skills—continents and oceans, scientific process, literature circles with short stories, study skills, following directions, peer mentoring, parts of speech, writing summaries, visual tracking exercises
October	Writing planners and expanders, outlines, reading logs, keyboarding, taxonomy project, monster reports, landforms, parts of a newspaper
November	Cultural awareness, logic boxes, student progress conferences, food collections, persuasive essays, two-digit multiplication, *I Got a D in Salami*, Election Day coverage, structural analysis, listening activity, reassess math and reading levels
December	Poetry unit, *Phantom Tollbooth*, cooperative catalog math/holiday shopping groups, community projects, creating mnemonics, plant unit, how geography influences cultures, portfolios reviewed, winter word problems, parent-teacher conferences
January	Class graphs of favorites, science vocabulary picture books, social studies centers on geographic regions, *Old Yeller* reading groups, New Year's resolutions, decimals and percentages, *Time for Kids*, current events—local and national
February	Heart bulletin board, figurative language, idioms, analogies, fraction unit, technology centers, colonial projects, vertebrates and invertebrates, current events—international articles, computer language tools, reassess math and reading levels
March	Tessellations, probability, graphs, inventions, women in history, Dr. Seuss books, American Revolution play, how to cite sources, reading skills with *Beethoven Lives Upstairs*, review meanings of prefixes, current events—sports and entertainment, parent-teacher conferences
April	Architecture unit, lights and shadows, geometry unit, review all computational skills, branches of government, Bill of Rights, *The Lion, the Witch & the Wardrobe*, oral discussions about World War II, share pen pal correspondence, interactive character writing
May	Hands-on algebraic equations, classroom newspaper, Holocaust unit (*Terrible Things, The Upstairs Room*), pet peeves and animals around the world, forces and shapes in nature
June	*Hatchet*, biography reports, exercise logs, sports and art math centers, area and perimeter, compare and contrast governments around the world, reassess math and reading levels
July	Biome and environment units: beaches, rainforests, coral reefs, forests, mountains, grasslands, deserts, freshwater, marine, tundra; math PowerPoints; reading logs reviewed; class newspapers published; social studies world games created and shared; curriculum songs in math, science, reading, and social studies; self-assessments on portfolios

Figure 6.3 Algebra II

First Quarter Goals and Objectives

Algebra 1 Skills: To review skills acquired from Algebra I and apply the skills to a variety of problems.

Goal Logs: To create a log proclaiming what each student wants to achieve in Algebra II and how they plan to accomplish these goals.

Equations and Inequalities: To simplify and evaluate algebraic expressions, solve linear and absolute value equations, and solve and graph inequalities.

Linear Relations and Functions: To identify, graph, and write linear equations.

Real-World Problems: To incorporate real-world applications into linear relations and functions.

Scatter Plots: To draw scatter plots and find prediction equations.

Social/Behavior: To follow all classroom and schools rules with academics and behavior, and have a mutual respect between teachers and students.

Study Skills: To organize work in a binder with different sections for homework, notes, and class work.

Second Quarter Goals and Objectives

Systems of Equations and Inequalities: To solve systems of linear equations in two or three variables and solve systems of inequalities.

Graphing: To model systems of equations by graphing and explore technology by using a graphing calculator to check the work.

Linear Programming: To use linear programming to find minimum and maximum values of functions.

Matrices: To organize data in matrices, perform operations with matrices and determinants, and use matrices to solve systems of equations.

Microsoft Excel: To input data correctly into Microsoft Excel and perform basic operations on the data, e.g. mean, median, mode.

Quadratic Functions and Inequalities: To graph and solve quadratic functions, perform operations with complex numbers, and graph and solve quadratic inequalities.

Social/Behavior: To use collaboration skills worked on in the first quarter to successfully complete tasks and projects with peers.

Study Skills: To use study tools such as 3-D systems of equations, Foldables study organizer, and key words.

Third Quarter Goals and Objectives

Polynomial Functions: To add, subtract, multiply, divide, and factor polynomials and to evaluate polynomial functions and solve polynomial equations.

(Continued)

Figure 6.3 (Continued)

Radical Equations and Inequalities: To find the composition of functions, determine the inverses of function or relations, and to simplify and solve equations involving roots, radicals, and rational exponents.
Operations on Functions: To find the sum, difference, product, and quotient of functions.
Dimensional Analysis: To analyze word problems and convert the information into the appropriate form.
Rational Expressions and Equations: To simplify rational expressions and solve direct, joint, and inverse variation problems.
Graphing: To analyze and graph polynomial functions and rational functions.
Social/Behavior: To continue to work successfully in collaborative groups and monitor any unfavorable behavior still persisting.
Study Skills: To use real-world problems and examples to connect concepts to procedures.
Fourth Quarter Goals and Objectives
Exponential and Logarithmic Relations: To simplify exponential and logarithmic expressions; solve exponential and logarithmic equations and inequalities; and solve problems involving exponential growth and decay.
Word Problems: To create real-world problems involving exponents and quadratic systems.
Quadratic Systems: To solve systems of quadratic equations algebraically and graphically, and solve systems of quadratic inequalities graphically.
Sequences and Series: To use arithmetic and geometric sequences and series.
Conic Sections: To write and graph equations of parabolas, circles, ellipses, and hyperbolas.
Self-Assessments: To evaluate the performance and information learned in Algebra II and how it will be applied to real life.
Social/Behavior: To continue to exhibit restraint and focus from the beginning of the quarter until the end.
Study Skills: To organize information learned into relevance by comparing and contrasting.

Long Range Monthly Plans: Algebra II Inclusive

August	Review IEPs and 504s with teams and share accommodations with all staff, Complete family contact sheet for all classes, Back-to-School night, School rules, Review of Algebra 1 skills/assessment of prior knowledge, Goal logs, Universal binder organization
September	Start first degree equations and inequalities unit, Equations and Inequalities, study skills, following directions, collaborative skills, Algebra labs, real-world problems, number lines to solve absolute value equations, graphing calculator activity
October	Linear relations and functions, Graphing, Domain and range, Reading math activity, Real-world slope graphing on calculator and on paper, Slope project, Scatter plots, Special functions, Key words, Contact with parents/guardians when necessary
November	Systems of equations and inequalities, Foldables study organizer, Graphing, Graphs to algebra, Number tile project, Methods charts, Linear programming, Word problems containing systems of equations, 3-D Systems of equations in three variables: paper activity, Standardized test prep
December	Matrices, Organizing data, using Microsoft excel to manipulate data, Transformations, Cramer's rule, Using matrices to solve systems of equations, Holiday excel spreadsheets
January	Review of key terms from previous lessons, Review initial goals, Linking it together project, Start Quadratic, Polynomial, and Radical Equations and Inequalities unit, Quadratic Functions and Inequalities, Sports graphing, complex numbers, Completing the square lab, Analyzing graphs of quadratic functions, graphing calculator lab: modeling motion
February	Polynomial functions, properties of exponents, exponents in science, reading math: dimensional analysis, Dividing polynomials book jacket, Honeycomb activity, analyzing graphs/standardized test prep, rational zero theorem, Start radical equations and inequalities
March	Continue radical equations and inequalities, operations on functions, Inverses of functions lab, Bridge square root activity, graphing calculation lab with square roots, Mona Lisa warm-up
April	Start advanced functions and relations unit, rational expressions and equations, study organizer, adding and subtracting rational expressions, Mirror and lens project, graphing rational functions, Real-world word problems, classes of functions lesson and matching activity, Ipod problem
May	Exponential and logarithmic relations, teams in a basketball tournament, modeling data using exponential functions, Base e and natural logarithms, calculator tutorial, (logarithms), Reading math double meaning activity, growth and decay
June	Conic sections, colored index cards, matching activities, quadratic systems, Sequences and series, sequences and series in real life, Excel lab: Loans and interest, Mathematical induction
July	Proving algebra, Review of initial goals, self-assessments, interest projects, Tying it all together game, real-world assessments

Source: Designed by Allison Boehm. Used with permission.

Figure 6.4 Physics Class Quarterly Plans

First Quarter Goals and Objectives
Math: Ensure all students have the fundamentals of algebra and significant figures (digits)
Math: How to analyze and generate graphs
General Science: Metric units, including prefixes and MLK (meters, liters, kilograms), the base units used in physics
General Science: The scientific method and good experimental practices in physics
Physics: Mechanics, specifically: distance, velocity, and acceleration
Perceptual: "To attend to teachers and peers, filtering out distracting stimuli"
Social/Behavioral: To create and follow a student-generated set of rules for behavior and academics, ex: HW, attention, time on task
Study Skills: To organize upcoming work in an assignment planner for HW, tests, projects, etc.
Second Quarter Goals and Objectives
Lab Skills: Create an experiment with appropriate independent and dependent variables for what is desired to be tested
Analytical: Ability to analyze data gathered in a lab setting to generate a physics formula
Reading/writing: Scientific writing skills ex: proper terminology and descriptions
Math: Focus on proportionality (direct, inverse, etc), focus on more advanced algebra skills
Physics: Lab-generated formulas for angular motion and forces in general
Physics: Newton's Laws of motion and how they apply (as does all of physics) to the real world around us
Social/Behavior: Work cooperatively in groups (for labs and otherwise) with specific roles that rotate
Study Skills: To create your own study guides from various notes and handouts
Third Quarter Goals and Objectives
Study Skills: To create your own study guides from various notes and handouts
Reading: Increase abilities with interpreting and solving word problems
Physics: Energy; solving mechanics problems with energy
Physics: Applying energy and forces to electromagnetism

Science: Apply physics principles to student's designs and student's interests
Research: Scientific research practices and writing skills
Social/Behavior: Work as a fully autonomous and highly functional group
Study Skills: Combine cumulative knowledge gained and applying to new topics
Fourth Quarter Goals and Objectives
Physics: Optics, waves, and modern physics
Science: Reinforce the importance of "science by doing"
Skills: Critical thinking skills as well as logical thinking
Writing: Write a design proposal and scientific paper
Practical: Going from the design to creation phase of a project
Technology: Utilization of laboratory and graphing software
Interdisciplinary: Using skills developed in other classes in physics, and skills gained here in other classes and the real world
Study Skills: Creating study guides to create an end product

Long Range Monthly Plans: Physics

August	Review IEPs and 504s with teams and share accommodations with all staff, school rules, assess math facts, class rules developed, lab group jobs and setup established
September	Review fundamental math and algebra skills, introduce the concepts of significant figures, review the metric system and introduce the base units of physics (meters, liters, and kilograms)
October	Introduction to mechanics, applying distance and velocity to the real world (sports, driving, etc.), utilizing labs and probes to strengthen these
November	Acceleration tied in, utilization of distance vs. time graphs and velocity vs. time graphs, graphical analysis utilized
December	Develop experiment to discover Newton's second law of motion, emphasize importance of independent, dependent variables and controls in experiments, development of Newton's other laws
January	Utilization of angular motion experiment to develop multiple physical principles and formulas, applying Newton's Laws to angular motion with tie-ins to the real world

(Continued)

Figure 6.4 (Continued)

February	Free body diagrams to solve complex problems, introduction to energy with key concepts of conservation of energy, and relationship between energy and forces
March	Energy utilized to demonstrate the relationship between different forms of energy and mechanical processes in the world and universe at large
April	Electromagnetism studied with links drawn between electricity and physics on the atomic level, inverse squared relationship studied and related to other forces
May	Optics studied, laboratory experiments utilizing lenses, prisms, polar lenses, etc., to study the properties of light, the particle-wave duality introduced
June	Wave mechanics introduced, music utilized for concepts such as harmonics, physical properties effects on waves established, Final project presentations on physics concepts
July	Modern physics introduced, special relativity presented to correct the paradox of Newtonian physics and the speed of light being constant, relationship of physics to nuclear radiation and other nuclear topics

Source: Designed by Michael Kleeman. Used with permission.

84

Figure 6.5 Quarterly Lesson Plan Units

Include social, emotional, behavioral, technology, and study skills as appropriate.

First-Quarter Goals and Objectives	Second-Quarter Goals and Objectives
Third-Quarter Goals and Objectives	Fourth-Quarter Goals and Objectives

Instructional Materials:

Long Range Monthly Plans

August	
September	
October	
November	
December	
January	
February	
March	
April	
May	
June	
July	

discussions to formulate inclusion action plans that avoid a gap between the intended curriculum and what students actually learn. Access to the general education curriculum involves infusing appropriate research-based instruction, materials, accommodations, and assessments.

Teacher instructional approaches are reviewed to offer students both the information and challenges. For example, replacing lecturing with more facilitation to encourage higher-level thinking skills through appropriately leveled questioning is a valuable way to ensure that students are learning, rather than memorizing unrelated facts. The degree of scaffolding is individualized depending on learner needs and levels. By reviewing student progress, appropriate inclusion decisions are collaboratively formulated in terms of which curriculum standards need to be reviewed and enriched. As mentioned before, UDL offers additional supports and services for the participation of students with disabilities in general education classrooms. These neuroscience principles offer multiple ways for learners to understand the curriculum. This aspect of UDL offers a broad range of goals, methods, materials, and assessments for all students. Preparing teachers for how to deliver the curriculum in their classrooms using UDL principles requires training. The Center for Applied Special Technology (2012) offers ideas, but experts in the field note that teachers need to be given the planning time and professional development to then align the general education curriculum standards to individual student needs, with interventions such as differentiation of instruction and UDL.

School principals, leaders, and coaches are often the role models whose attitudes and beliefs influence both teacher and student performance. The administration needs to reaffirm positive attitudes toward the general education classroom placement by communicating messages that support high outcomes for all learners. Offering educators and all staff this ongoing support occurs in ongoing formal and informal coaching conversations.

Scope, sequence, and *rigor* are not terms that are exclusive to students without disabilities. Ricki Sabia (personal communication, April 3, 2012), associate director of the National Down Syndrome Society National Policy Center and the parent of a child with Down syndrome, makes this salient point:

> I'm tired of people asking why he should learn Shakespeare, when he can't even tie his shoes! Maybe he'll be an usher in a theater that has Shakespearean plays. These kids can do more than the basic stuff, and that can be taught in the context of the academics. Why can't reading and following directions be taught in a biology or chemistry class?

COMMON CORE STATE STANDARDS: ENGLISH LANGUAGE ARTS AND MATH CURRICULUM STANDARDS

The Council Chief State School Officers and National Governors Association (2012) developed the Common Core State Standards (CCSS). The CCSS currently outline the knowledge and skills students in Grades K–12 are expected to learn in English language arts (ELA) and mathematics. There are fewer and clearer standards that are intended to provide students with deeper learning experiences. The idea is for states to communicate with one another and to have high expectations for all students. With uniform national standards, students who move from state to state will not face disparate learning.

If multiplying and dividing fractions is taught in fifth grade in New York, New Mexico students are doing the same math at the same grade level. To date, nearly all states have agreed that there is a set of knowledge that students need to have in reading, writing, language arts, listening and speaking, and mathematics. This set of skills is intended to help all students become college and career ready to compete in a global market.

Districts across the nation are concerned about CCSS implementation for all students, including those with disabilities. Current concerns include whether most states will have the funding in this time of budget cuts for training or for purchasing new curriculum materials, how special education students' unique needs are addressed, and the need for more clarity with modifications for assessments. Educators need direction to apply and strengthen the standards for students who are learning together with their peers within inclusive classrooms. In order to reach a variety of student levels, teachers' lessons need to connect the standards with instruction that honors students' differing levels. That is why it is crucial that appropriate interventions and supports be available to allow learners performing below or above grade levels and English learners the opportunities to proficiently access the knowledge and skills.

School leaders, administrators, and coaches help educators within inclusive classrooms by reviewing the data and observing students and teachers during lessons. This includes offering effective classroom management tips, core materials, resources, and ideas for appropriate instruction and assessments that help students to achieve the standards in each grade. Modeling, scaffolding, reinforcing, strengthening, and enriching the standards with unique practices is part of the inclusive process. The education standards list grade-level academic expectations, with the idea that students who receive special education services are general education students first. How students with disabilities who attend elementary and secondary schools across our nation will achieve the rigorous core standards, minus the challenges, is not yet defined, according to many education experts and stakeholders.

The language of the standards cannot be interpreted literally but must be appropriate for specific groups of learners. For example, the standards ask students to *explain, watch, listen, speak,* or *draw.* A student with an intellectual disability may be challenged to *explain* the theme of a novel, while a student who is blind cannot *watch* a video, nor would a student who is deaf *listen* to a story read orally. A student with a severe communication or language difficulty could not *speak* about the steps taken to solve a math equation, and a student with dysgraphia or a fine motor physical impairment will have difficulty *drawing* a scene from a book read. School leaders need to help educators learn how to integrate the CCSS into existing systems with appropriate interventions to organize that inclusive classroom to improve student outcomes. In this case, the literal language needs to be translated into pragmatic inclusive scenarios.

Several more CCSS details need to be ironed out. Two consortiums are undertaking how students are assessed. The Partnership for Assessment of Readiness for College and Careers (PARCC) and the Smarter Balanced Assessment Consortium (SBAC) are designing online assessments with the availability of components such as speech to text, foreground and background color options, tactile approaches (e.g., Braille), and bigger fonts built in. Item and task assessment types include selected-response items, technology-enhanced items, constructed-response items, and performance tasks. Assessments are slated to be available for the 2014–2015 school year. School leaders, educators, and all stakeholders want these assessments to consistently be appropriate ones that align with the standards. It is important to note that the standards do not replace students' IEPs. Local education teams make IEP decisions in terms of modifications and accommodations. However, states will need to choose general and alternative assessments with consistency and parity. Districts also need to have the money to purchase computers, and many are concerned with how the computerized assessments impact instruction.

The standards do not matter much if they sit on a shelf, according to a 2012 *Education Week* commentary, which cites the findings of a study of the CCSS, *The 2012 Brown Center Report on American Education* (Loveless, 2012a, 2012b). Solid curriculum, excellent teaching and assessment practices, and accountability systems matter more, according to Tom Loveless (2012), the author of the *Brown Center Report*. Past studies referenced denote that the quality of former curriculum standards had little effect on student achievement. According to Loveless, the effectiveness of the curriculum and strategies is the primary criterion.

Students with and without disabilities need to read, write, and do math. The CCSS tell educators what will be learned, but they do not offer specific ways on how students will accomplish the skills and knowledge. Accessibility, accountability, and high expectations are applicable for students with disabilities, but no one has really explained how students of all ability levels will achieve the CCSS.

In the 1940s, George Reavis, assistant superintendent of schools in Cincinnati, Ohio, wrote a parable about a school for animals that offered the subjects of running, climbing, flying, and swimming. All of the animals took all of the subjects, but problems arose when the deer was great at running, but not swimming, and the duck was excellent at swimming, but failed running. The moles ended up dropping out of school to start a private school with the rabbits because they wanted digging and burrowing added to the curriculum. The parable questions whether one size fits all. Today, the CCSS are offered for all students, including students with disabilities. Some groups embrace and applaud these efforts, while others question whether students with disabilities will be challenged or become scapegoats for schools that do not achieve progress. School leaders now must ensure that educators deliver appropriate accommodations within the inclusive classroom to scaffold individual learners' unique needs and levels.

Currently, the CCSS are denoted for ELA and mathematics. The CCSS are intended to increase academic rigor for all students. Students are encouraged to read more complex texts, like detectives, to search for answers and document their understanding. This includes comprehending fiction genres with diverse literature selections and achieving greater skills to provide textual evidence in nonfiction and informational text. Writers are asked to compose expository, persuasive, and argumentative pieces, taking the writing many steps beyond personal essays. Communication skills in listening and speaking involve coherently expressing ideas, thoughts, and feelings. In mathematics there are set standards of practice for Grades K–12 that want students to make sense of problems, persevere in solving them, think abstractly, and use logical reasoning, arguments, models, tools, and structure. It is important to reiterate as stated on the CCSS website (see Council of Chief State School Officers & National Governors Association, 2012) that the standards do not tell teachers how to teach. However, with a greater emphasis on critical thinking skills, teachers must now ask questions that lead students to become critical thinkers. Overall, the standards focus more on results than means. More specifics for ELA and mathematics follow. (A mobile app is also available from MasteryConnect, 2012.)

CCSS ELA

The CCSS for English Language Arts (ELA) delineate reading, writing, listening and speaking, and language standards. There are common threads in the ELA standards that overlap for instruction and assessments with many ways that the reading, writing, and communication standards connect to students of all ability levels. There is a range of complexity in the quality and quantity of readings and writings with informational and fictional texts. Headings for literature and informational text include skills with key ideas and details, craft and structure, integration of knowledge and ideas, and a range of readings and levels of complexity. Students are expected to be fluent readers who read with purpose, understanding, accuracy, appropriate rate, expression, and self-recognition to support their comprehension. Students are encouraged to go beyond summarizations to continually analyze and support what they read and write with text-based details, facts, and information.

Writing standards include students who give information, reactions, details, descriptions, points of view, and research to build and present knowledge. The speaking and listening strands include headings such as comprehension, collaboration, and presentation of knowledge and ideas. The language strands involve conventions of Standard English, knowledge of language, and vocabulary acquisition and use. Grades K–5 emphasize literacy in history, social studies, science, and technical subjects within the reading domains, while Grades 6–12 relate literacy in history, social studies, science, and technical subjects with college and career readiness (CCR) expectations and more specificity.

Inclusive classrooms must be welcoming ones for all learners. Educators need the resources and time to make this work for students who possess differing reading, writing, language, and speaking and listening skills. This involves reaching learners with lower levels to understand complex text and

Figure 6.6   Applying the CCSS for English Language Arts to Inclusive Classrooms

	Reading	Writing	Speaking and Listening	Language
Standards-Based Lesson Objectives	Generate written and verbal responses to text-dependent questions	Write for an audience and stress the use of evidence to inform and make arguments	Clearly express ideas, thoughts, and feelings in an organized presentation	Sort words into their parts of speech and use these words in writings and speech
Whole Class Lesson	Choral reading of text followed by Socratic discussion, and assignments that include dialectical dialogue, storyboards, comic strips, and student-created skits	Interactive editing skills with writing rubric and models provided to students who write argumentative pieces with supporting facts, definitions, and appropriate vocabulary	Moving debate on specific topics (e.g., whether school should have a yearlong calendar, and whether or not schools should have a dress code)	Group lesson on nouns, verbs, adjectives, and adverbs, with a BrainPOP introduction and an interactive class quiz.
Small Groups	Scaffolding for students with close monitoring of guided reading group's skills to cite and paraphrase key ideas in text; content-related visuals will be provided; intermittent checks of all groups as teachers and assistants circulate and offer feedback	Cooperative writing for different audiences, based on the same prompt; students interface to revise as peer editors and writing mentors; strategy table available with tools and scaffolding that includes electronic dictionaries, thesauruses, transitional word lists, and writing frames	Interest-driven groups present opinions in collaborative speeches; assessment is a checklist to self-reflect (e.g., organization, clarity, volume, body language, visuals); peers and teachers also offer feedback with reciprocal teaching	Assignments are given based on the results of an informal online quiz, review of adjectives and adverbs on computer program Grammar Jammers; as skills are mastered, students join class scavenger hunt to categorize items found to matching parts of speech; groups are then given the choice to write poems, speeches, and short stories that use these parts of speech
Individual Students	Five students are provided with lower-level reading text to gain the same skills; a few students use the AutoSummarize tool to check their understanding; three students read passages with vocabulary at a higher level	Teacher conferences with students performing at, on, and above level to offer writing feedback for revisions and reflections; extra time to complete the assignment is offered with a schedule of completion dates for the substeps given	One student has different communicative skills and cannot participate within a group; student has a peer mentor and visually expresses functional speech on an iPad using TouchChat application	Some students are offered a morphology chart with color-coded words matched to the correct part of speech; a few students use the text-to-speech tool and the computer dictionary tools

challenging students with higher levels. The idea is to support, not frustrate or bore, students. Classrooms that are stocked with appropriately leveled texts across the genres are prepared to provide students with opportunities for clarification, repetition, application, generalization, and enrichment. Resources range from graphic novels to e-zines, historical fiction, plays, informational texts, technical readings, fables, folktales, advertisements, editorials, comparative essays, and more. It is important that educators also be coached with practices that value both UDL and RTI to vary their goals, methods, materials, assessments, and classroom grouping. Coaching teachers to provide learners with the appropriate interventions and providing educators with the time to review the data for all groups of learners are essential. Figure 6.6 offers principals, school leaders, coaches, and educators ideas on how the ELA standards are applied to specific lesson objectives for whole class, small group, and individual instruction, valuing the principles of UDL and RTI.

The Common Core State Standards for English Language Arts are available online from the Council of Chief State School Officers and the National Governors Association (2012). View the following sites and resources for additional CCSS ELA insights for whole-class, small-group, and individual reading for independent and interactive reading opportunities and assignments across ability levels (Karten, 2012a):

http://www.readingrockets.org/

http://www.primarygames.com/reading.php

http://www.rif.org/

http://www.alline.org/euro/ereading.html

https://www.bookshare.org/

www.learningally.org

www.kidspiration.com

http://quizlet.com

http://www.scholastic.com/kids/homework/flashcards.htm

CCSS Mathematics

The math standards for Grades K–8 are organized in domains, while the standards for 9th–12th graders are organized by conceptual categories. Grades K–5 include the domains of counting and cardinality, operations and algebraic thinking, numbers and operations in base 10, numbers and operations with fractions (Grades 3–5), measurement and data, and geometry. Grades 6–8 include knowing the number systems, geometry, statistics and probability, ratios and proportional relationships (6–7), expressions, equations, and functions (8). High school expectations include knowing number and quantity, algebra, functions, geometry, statistics and probability, and modeling across all categories. Figure 6.7 lists the eight CCSS standards of mathematical practice for educators of students in Grades K–12 to review. The goal is for students to continually increase expertise with these mathematical processes and proficiencies to increase their understandings of both procedures and concepts. The applicable scenarios invite you to think of other ways to incorporate these eight practices in math lessons and across the curriculum.

Figure 6.7   Eight CCSS Standards of Mathematical Practice: Grades K–12

CCSS Standards for Mathematical Practice	Inclusion Scenarios
1. Make sense of problems and persevere in solving them.	A fourth grader solves a math problem by dividing and saying that 24½ students will be traveling on each bus. He or she needs to stop to realize and reflect that this answer does not make sense.
2. Reason abstractly and quantitatively.	A student knows the total two-day revenue achieved at a concert and the amount generated for one of the days, and then is able to write a linear equation that uses the variable x to solve for the amount generated on the other day.
3. Construct viable arguments and critique the reasoning of others.	Student communicates understandings to peers by creating a logic box to solve a word problem.
4. Model with mathematics.	Cooperative groups of students use actual restaurant menus to find out the cost each one will contribute to the bill if the total meal of student-selected items is evenly divided with tax and tip.
5. Use appropriate tools strategically.	Students use visual fraction models from National Council of Teachers of Mathematics (2012) site to compare fractions, mixed numbers, decimals, and percentages.
6. Attend to precision.	Students carefully label x and y axes as they plot coordinates on graph paper to determine the slope of a line by looking at the ratio of the change in y to the change in x.
7. Look for and make use of structure.	Students sort shapes according to the number of sides.
8. Look for and express regularity in repeated reasoning.	Students examine 100s charts to see patterns with 10 more, and other addition and subtraction patterns (e.g., $4 + 9 = 13$, $14 + 9 = 23$, $24 + 9 = 33$; $16 − 7 = 9$, $26 − 7 = 19$, $36 − 7 = 29$).
Teachers are invited to apply one or more of these eight standards to build student competencies.	

The mathematical standards are intended to help students increase declarative, procedural, and conceptual knowledge. Each grade builds on and expands prior skills and knowledge with increasing proficiency. For example, a first grader uses his or her knowledge of place value and the properties of operations to add and subtract within 20, while third graders use place value and the properties of operations to perform multidigit arithmetic. Mathematics is more than the memorization of facts or information to pass tests, but it involves creating strong foundations in Grades K–5 to pave the way for in-depth algebraic reasoning and numerous life applications. Middle school students have stronger learning in geometry, algebra, probability, and statistics, while high school students continually add to this learning to link math and statistics to everyday life, work, and decision making.

Inclusion coaches assist educators in determining appropriate instructional strategies that help students with differing needs solidify the procedures and concepts. For example, a student who does not remember his or her multiplication facts or has perceptual issues will consequently have difficulties with two-digit multiplication and long division. Teachers would need knowledge of and access to a multitude of VAKT approaches and guidance to select and offer supportive strategies, resources, and programs to strengthen that student's multiplication fluency. If students lack a conceptual understanding of the multiplication process, then direct skill instruction and practice with arrays, repeated addition, skip counting, multiples, and basic facts with graph paper, online flashcards, or computer sites and other resources are required. Coaching recommendations offer educators strategies for helping students gain the prerequisite skills to solve more intricate problems to gain proficiencies. Professionals in learning teams collaboratively brainstorm and share strategies such as color coding the digits to highlight place value, using base-10 blocks as manipulatives, increasing verbalization, and offering the learner outlined written steps or cue cards to follow to strengthen procedural, conceptual, and/ or perceptual skills. Curriculum application of standards-based activities helps students develop increased skills with number sense and numerical operations. For example, students work collaboratively to discover an assortment of arrays and create their own problems with different array arrangements, rather than working with repeated worksheets. Incorporating technology along with multisensory approaches in mathematics is also essential and can include a range of tools, including those offered on these sites (Karten 2012b):

http://www.math-play.com/

http://www.scholastic.com/kids/homework/flashcards.htm

www.funbrain.com

http://www.touchmath.com/

The *Common Core State Standards for Mathematics* is available online from the Council of Chief State School Officers and the National Governors Association (2012). These next sites offer more illustrations and resources (Karten, 2012b):

http://www.nctm.org

http://www.insidemathematics.org

http://commoncoretools.me/illustrative-mathematics/

http://www.mathedleadership.org

http://commoncoretools.me

http://www.dyscalculia.org

http://www.techmatrix.org

http://mathspecialists.org

http://www.singaporemath.com/

http://www.ixl.com/

www.mathforum.org/library

Each inclusion class presents students with a variety of abilities, levels, and profiles. Sometimes educators require coaching to learn more about quality instruction rather than overloading the students with rapidly fired curriculum standards. School leaders, educators, and coaches exchange ideas and collaboratively develop plans to move forward so that the curriculum standards are applicable for each and every student. The learning is multiplied for all when teachers are coached to follow a step-by-step approach to infuse the standards into their lessons.

A Recommended Step-by-Step Approach for Implementing the CCSS

Step 1: Review math, reading, writing, speaking and listening, and language standards from prior, current, and following years.

Step 2: Slate topics for each quarter, month, and week for class, small groups, and individual students.

Step 3: Share the standards with learners in student-friendly language.

Step 4: Create a task analysis of a standard that includes visuals and graphic organizers. Monitor student progress.

Step 5: Revisit and adjust whole class, small groups, and individual student lessons based on formal and informal assessments, and IEP objectives.

Source: Adapted from Karten, T. (2012). *Common Core Standards: Unique practices for inclusive classrooms: English language arts (Laminated guide).* Port Chester, NY: National Professional Resources, Dude Publishing.

The IDEA Partnership offers materials about the core standards to help administrators and their educators in school districts make the transition to the Common Core State Standards. Some of the resources and services include dialogue guides for groups such as educators and parents who may have differing prior knowledge. Virtual mentoring is also offered. As more curriculum standards are incorporated, more training, support, and coaching are recommended. Information can be accessed online (see National Association of State Directors of Special Education, n.d.).

CROSS-DISCIPLINARY APPROACHES

A way that coaches help educators guide their students to accomplish 21st century skills within inclusive environments is through project-based and interdisciplinary learning. This real-life application across themes integrates the concepts, skills, disciplines, and experiences. Project-based learning allows students to demonstrate what they have learned with in-depth investigation of subject areas. Hands-on projects build skills such as increased collaboration and communication, along with increased student motivation. The curriculum has increased relevance, whether students are investigating the Chesapeake Bay, visiting a senior center, or growing, cooking, buying, advertising, or selling snacks for a school store. Students are empowered when they are given real-world learning choices that relate to their interests and skills.

Cross-disciplinary units allow students and teachers to collaborate between content and units. A high school English teacher who is planning a lesson about Latin prefixes is encouraged to share his or her lesson objective with the algebra, geometry, world history, art, music, physical education, biology, earth science, and chemistry teachers to allow the vocabulary to connect across subjects. Elementary and secondary teachers focus on specific themes and/or processes, whether instructing about neighborhoods, fractions, photosynthesis, the English Renaissance, nutrition, civil disobedience, social justice, ladybugs, or global warming. When lessons are cross-disciplinary, the learning is continued from one room or subject to the next, with a set of outlined objectives across the disciplines. This assists students in connecting information with pragmatic skills as they hear additional perspectives. Repetition through different contexts then solidifies the learning.

In addition, each teacher is usually an expert in his or her content area, especially middle school and high school teachers along with art, music, physical education, theater, and dance educators. However, students often receive fragmented knowledge instead of seeing how the learning is connected across the subjects. Themes connect the learning from one subject or room to the next within elementary classrooms and across middle school and high school subjects. As an example, if a team of teachers chose the theme of *changes*, that would connect to the metamorphosis of a butterfly or global warming in a science class, technological changes in the Industrial Revolution, point perspective in art, or changing coefficient values in algebraic equations. This way *changes* are better understood! Sharing each educator's strengths and expertise then occurs across the disciplines.

The planner in Figure 6.8 invites educators to share their lessons with each other to tap into one another's strengths, insights, and collaborative expertise.

Ultimately, school is the place that prepares students and provides them with the skills to live independent productive adult lives, but first the inclusive classroom is infused with unique practices for each and every student to have access to the knowledge. As the next section denotes, educators need to be privy to the many inclusion factors and receive support from coaches to continually improve each and every student's learning experiences within that inclusive classroom.

Figure 6.8 Let's Do This Together: Cross-Curricular Planner to Strengthen Connections

This week our class is learning about:

Let's collaborate and connect our lessons.

Teacher(s)/Classes:

Lesson/unit:

Dates:

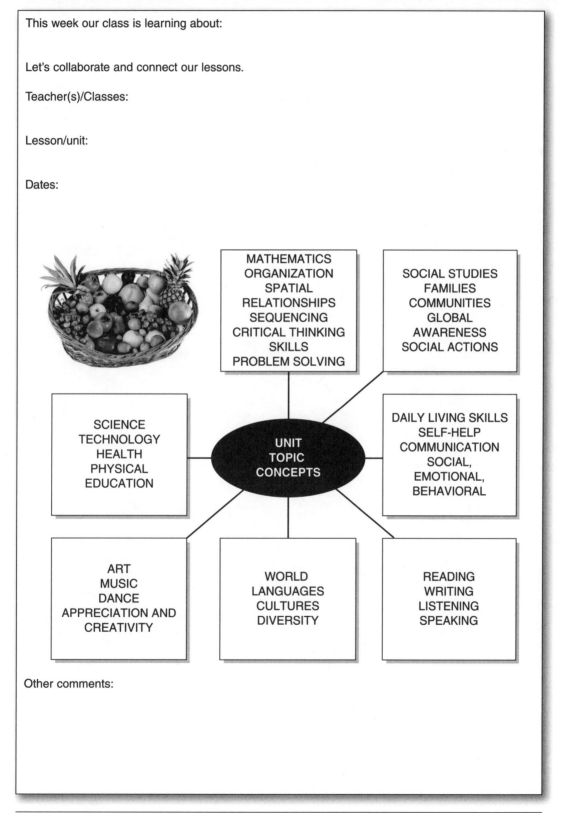

MATHEMATICS
ORGANIZATION
SPATIAL
RELATIONSHIPS
SEQUENCING
CRITICAL THINKING
SKILLS
PROBLEM SOLVING

SOCIAL STUDIES
FAMILIES
COMMUNITIES
GLOBAL
AWARENESS
SOCIAL ACTIONS

SCIENCE
TECHNOLOGY
HEALTH
PHYSICAL
EDUCATION

UNIT
TOPIC
CONCEPTS

DAILY LIVING SKILLS
SELF-HELP
COMMUNICATION
SOCIAL,
EMOTIONAL,
BEHAVIORAL

ART
MUSIC
DANCE
APPRECIATION AND
CREATIVITY

WORLD
LANGUAGES
CULTURES
DIVERSITY

READING
WRITING
LISTENING
SPEAKING

Other comments:

Source: Adapted from Karten, T. (2010c). *Inclusion strategies that work! Research-based methods for the classroom.* Thousand Oaks, CA: Corwin.

PART III

Strengths and Challenges of Inclusion

7

Inclusion Matters

INCLUSION YEAS AND NAYS

At times administrators and educators alike are frustrated by time and scheduling constraints, assessment demands, and an assortment of noneducational factors that influence daily inclusion decisions and classroom practices. Teachers possess differing thoughts about how inclusion works based on their prior experiences and school supports. Educators with successful experiences and strong administrative supports may be more receptive to the coaching process. Often the concept of inclusion is not challenged, but at times the implementation process is debated. Good instructional leaders manage many complexities and know that how things are done is often as important to success as what is being done (Bartalo, 2012).

Inclusion allows students more exposure to grade-level curriculum with students learning side-by-side with age-level peers as role models (Karten, 2010c). However, it is a challenging task for educators to simultaneously match their teaching practices with addressing standards, providing differentiation, and actively engaging all students (Killion, 2008).

During inclusion coaching sessions, teachers candidly shared a variety of concerns, with these being the major headings:

- Available common planning time/communication with colleagues
- Continuity of inclusion assignments from year to year
- Defining, sharing, and tweaking co-teaching responsibilities
- Pacing inclusion strategies without diluting lesson concepts

Both general and special educators are faced with the tasks of simultaneously teaching all students to mastery despite many student and curriculum variables—for example, prior knowledge, motivation, complexity of skills, topics, and classroom dynamics. Debates at the forefront include not sacrificing one group of students' needs over the needs of another group; dividing responsibilities among co-teachers; figuring out which accommodations help, but do not enable, students; and the lack of consistency with family and district support. Available planning time; communication with colleagues; continuity and division of inclusion assignments; defining, sharing, and tweaking co-teaching responsibilities; and the application of the inclusion strategies without diluting lessons and/or interfering with the curriculum pacing are all common issues that have been identified and shared by teachers as inclusive quagmires. Instead of focusing on these issues and allowing negativity to rule, inclusion coaches need to continually propagate good teaching practices via the inclusion strategies. Inclusion strategies are like the states of matter. They vary in intensity and substance at different age levels (Carpenter & Dyal, 2007; Mastropieri & Scruggs, 2001; Karten, 2010c, 2011). With proper administrative supports and highly trained staff, the inclusion strategies are applicable for all learners, without sacrificing one group of students or educators.

At times, the inclusion road is a bumpy one, since inclusion has its own set of skills that surface with student performance and behavior. Inclusion challenges often evolve as children's needs are revealed in response to the curriculum and lesson choices. Ignoring students is not an option, but appropriate interventions need to be applied to students who have difficulties (Ervin, 2008). Professionals who collaborate with each other figure out ways to help students achieve core standards within heterogeneous classrooms. Overall, the inclusion strengths lie within the system and individuals, and so do the challenges.

FUNDING ISSUES

District leaders are concerned about rising costs of special education services since many populations of students have increased in the past decade, including students with autism and children born prematurely who require specialized and often very costly services that take a chunk of money out of school budgets. How special education funding is spent is also often indeterminate within a complicated system (Samuels, 2011). The federal government covers approximately 17% of the costs, while districts and states shoulder the rest. Inclusive education is never a strategy for reducing costs. The main reason that a student is educated in an inclusive classroom is that general education classroom is determined to be his or her least restrictive environment. In addition, each state has a funding formula. Some states have a multiple-weights formula that offers more money based on the severity of a disability. This formula, everyone hopes, does not influence a district to place students in more restrictive environments if the placement is not an appropriate one. Other states use a census-based measure with equitable amounts distributed to districts based on assumptions about the number of students served and their classifications. The hazard here is that it is possible for districts to have inequitable proportions of students. As Rutgers University professor Bruce Baker notes in the Samuels (2011) article, districts are often at the mercy of what states are doing on their behalf.

Special education directors and other administrators in school districts across the nation always hope that the amount of federal contribution toward the cost of special education increases since it is very difficult to do more with less. However, sometimes it is a matter of just spending the money differently. Individuals with Disabilities Education Act (IDEA) dollars supplement state and local funds. Federal funds for IDEA have never come close to the amount authorized by the act, referred to as *full funding,* which is still only 40% of the average per pupil expenditure for all students. When funding declines, districts face difficult personnel decisions, which impact inclusion classroom realities. If special education staff numbers are reduced, then these layoffs result in greater class sizes, which lead to less-than-desirable student-teacher ratios. When districts reduce staff numbers, teachers, professional aides, and related staff are spread thinner with greater caseloads. The lack of money results in fewer staff and resources, which affects the quality of services since IDEA funds are often used to maintain and enhance services and programs.

Based on the IDEA formula, leaders in school districts are often challenged to find innovative ways to continue to provide free and appropriate public education to students with disabilities. IDEA grants often cover many costs of inclusion programs. This can range from using money to hire more personnel, training staff with more inservices, and hiring outside consultation and service providers to buying educational software or computers, books, and more. Districts allocate the money toward resources, programs, and services that enhance instruction to close achievement gaps. According to the U.S. Department of Education (2003), "Formula grant programs are noncompetitive awards based on a predetermined formula and are also referred to as state-administered programs. The OSEP-administered Individuals with Disabilities Education Act (IDEA) has three formula grant programs, the Grants to States program authorized by Part B Section 611 for children ages 3 through 21; the Preschool Grants program authorized by Part B Section 619 for children ages 3 through 5; and the Grants for Infants and Families program authorized by Part C for infants and toddlers, ages birth through 2 and their families." More information about applying for these grants is available from the U.S. Department of Education (n.d.).

Funding for an inclusion coach's services will vary and depend on whether the inclusion coach is an outside consultant or a district staff member. This can be applied to IDEA funding, grants, and allocations in district budgets. Some districts outsource services for transportation, janitorial, cafeteria, and secretarial services to lessen costs. Now, some districts have also begun to outsource special education services instead of exclusively having the services delivered by district personnel. This includes but is not limited to speech therapy services with distance learning and opportunities for student interactivity and hiring outside inclusion coaches, occupational therapists, instructional aides, and other related service providers. A few districts have also turned to private for-profit corporations that offer cost management and outside consulting to trim costs. Several districts are pleased with the results and savings obtained, and other school districts and parents question the quality and continuity of relationships (Schachter, 2012).

Other district leaders look at cost-effectiveness rather than cost reduction to fund special education programs (Levenson, 2011–2012) with academic return on investment (ROI). This includes deciding on academic supports and who should deliver them to maximize the achievements of a great number of students. Factors such as the effects on student learning, the number of students served, and the cost per child are investigated. It is not always the least expensive choice that is the best one. The article mentions that having a paraprofessional shadow a student with emotional needs in a general education class may be less expensive initially than hiring a behavioral interventionist, but in the long run the latter would be the wiser decision, since a trained behavioral interventionist could offer more strategies to several staff members at the same time and influence present and future students. Once the behavioral coping strategies are learned, they can be turnkeyed with other paraprofessionals and staff members. Thomas Parrish, director of the Center for Special Education Finance, a part of the American Institutes for Research, examined successful school districts and discovered that inclusion and the collaboration of general and special education are common factors in achieving higher test results for students who are educated in the general education classroom (Samuels, 2011). Parrish's research supports inclusion as not only a wise financial choice but a sound educational one as well.

Funding for special education programs and inclusive classrooms is a complex, but crucial, issue for all inclusion stakeholders to collaboratively iron out. It is vital that the data be carefully and collaboratively reviewed as opposed to making assumptions or following past practices. Just as there is differentiation of instruction, there is also differentiation of funding. Most important is that student achievement is put at the center of fiscal decisions.

8

Organization and Communication

SCHEDULING AND CLASS STRUCTURES

Research supports the idea that curricular modifications assist students in general education classes in increasing engagement with academic tasks, while at the same time decreasing classroom management issues (Lee, Wehmeyer, Soukup, & Palmer, 2010). The classroom environment, routines, and learning activities need to be rearranged to increase student engagement and on-task behavior (Epstein, Atkins, Cullinan, Kutash, & Weaver, 2008).

The challenges are to provide educators with ample time in their schedules and lower enough student-teacher ratios to plan lessons that address the levels of each and every student. Educators need frameworks that will afford them the structure to offer extra attention to all students—those who require remediation and those who need enrichment. Organization is also imperative for documenting schedules, strategies, interventions, and student progress. Inclusion teachers and monitoring teams need to review relevant data at specific intervals to decide whether to continue, tweak, and/or refine the interventions. Time to plan is an inclusion commodity that must be available to inclusive educators, support teams, and coaches before the school term begins, during the school day, and at ongoing professional development sessions. In addition, the inclusion classroom must be structured to communicate to the students and families that if co-teachers are present, the general and special education staff are equally responsible for all students.

Figure 8.1 offers examples and nonexamples of inclusion practices. Of course, each student and classroom presents its own specific levels and recommendations, but this figure offers a summary of effective strategies. Learning is enhanced when reflective teachers are treated as professionals.

Figure 8.1 Inclusion Structures for Educators and Students

Recommended Practices	Practices to Avoid and Delete
Establishing and posting classroom rules and routines with educator and student input and empowerment	Thrusting rules and routines upon teachers and the class without educator or student contributions and buy-in
Mapping out lessons for an entire unit of study and each marking period	Designing lessons day by day, without giving thought to the big picture
Allowing time in the year to repeat and review concepts and professional development (PD) in different ways	Moving on in the curriculum and PD, without thinking about retention and application
Welcoming each student and educator with a smile	Being a stress-filled leader, teacher, or coach
Posting lesson or coaching objectives at the beginning of a class or PD session and revisiting at close	Teaching and coaching without establishing lesson and PD purpose or reflecting upon outcomes
Listening and observing students' and educators' verbal and nonverbal communications	Missing the educator and student verbal and nonverbal cues and communications
Establishing prior educator and student knowledge with informal checks and Socratic discussion	Beginning lessons or PD sessions without student or educator input or time for educators to voice concerns
Creating a nonnegotiable pleasant classroom or PD learning environment	Implementing fast-paced, tension-filled classes and workshop sessions that cram learners with knowledge
Designing a variety of lessons, classroom stations, and PD opportunities that offer differentiated learning and support for whole groups and individuals	Lecturing for long classroom periods with few or little opportunities or scheduled time for independent or cooperative exploration, guided practice, application, or feedback
Composing attention-getting lessons and PD sessions that offer novelty (e.g., storytelling, humor, technology options, role-playing)	Repeating the same routines with little or no novelty with introduction, instruction, or reflections
Illustrating a sense of belonging by valuing student and educator contributions and efforts	No recognition for progress or efforts or treatment as integral learning partners
Applying meaningful tasks that relate the subject matter to student and educator interests	Exclusively teaching subjects and PD content without student or educator connections
Having high expectations for all students and educators with appropriate scaffolding and administrative supports to ensure outcomes	Thinking students and educators cannot learn; little or no accommodations, scaffolding, or administrative supports given
Honoring critical thinking skills with classroom applications	Concentrating on basic rote facts or research with no student or educator applications
Developing self-regulated learners who are aware of their strengths and weaknesses	Ignoring individual student and educator profiles and preferences
Offering timely corrective and specific feedback (e.g., praise, comments)	Allowing excessive time to pass before feedback is given (e.g., marking tests weeks later or not acknowledging educators' efforts)

GOALS AND PLANNING

The August–June schedule provided in Figure 8.2 offers annual goals for a K–6 school. This sample coaching schedule is followed in Figures 8.3 and 8.4 by educator communications that led to inclusion strategies and goals after informal classroom coaching observations and co-teaching sessions.

Figure 8.2 Inclusion Coaching: Our Goals for the Year

August–November

   a. Meet with administrators, team leaders, and coaches to review the data

   b. Share student, educator, family, and administrative inclusion needs and concerns

   c. Explore co-teaching models, staff collaboration, and instructional practices

   d. Develop lesson plans/timelines

   e. Decide on inclusion strategies and interventions for whole classes, small groups, and individual students

   f. Apply inclusion strategies and appropriate interventions

   g. Document implementation

November–February

   h. Meet with administrators, team leaders, coaches, educators, and related staff to review interventions

   i. Reflect on co-teaching and assistants' responsibilities and effectiveness to lower student-teacher ratios

   j. Tweak strategies, conduct interventions, and apply appropriate student scaffolding

   k. Continue to document effectiveness by monitoring and reviewing student data

February–April

   l. Meet with administrators, team leaders, coaches, and educators to review data on interventions

   m. Evaluate effectiveness of inclusion practices, co-teaching models, and collaborations

   n. Fine-tune inclusion strategies to match whole-class, small-group, and individual student, educator, and staff needs

April–June

   o. Meet with administrators, team leaders, coaches, and educators to review relevant data on interventions

   p. Fine-tune inclusion strategies and interventions

   q. Continue to document effectiveness

   r. Outline future plans for class schedules and teaching assignments

Figure 8.3 offers communications between an inclusion coach and K–6 teachers that yielded inclusion goals and strategies for improving classroom instruction and co-teaching practices.

Figure 8.3 Communications Between an Inclusion Coach and K–6 Teachers

Co-Teachers' Communications	Inclusion Strategies/Co-Teaching Plans and Goals Discussed
Kindergarten • Social/behavioral issues • Maturity level of students • Student application of rules and structure • Students feign buy-in for points with little internalization and empathy displayed • Students focus on negative in rules (e.g., no fighting, biting, shouting) • Begin with "divide and conquer" with math grouping • Groups have different perceptual, emotional, and attention needs	• Friendship behavioral point system structured with 1-2-3 continuum • Classroom rules revisited and stated in positive terms • Parallel co-teaching models with writing/English language arts small groups/one-to-one • Add classroom stations/centers (e.g., sensory, art, music) • Visual self-regulation chart with smiley face descriptors • Conference with individual students to review academic, emotional, social, and behavioral progress with expectations and respect honored • Model appropriate behavior with teachers and peers • Highlight importance of routines • Review *Functional Counting Skills* article from Council for Exceptional Children in reference to math lesson (Xin & Holmdal, 2003). • Continue to explore thematic lessons (e.g., respect, helping with character/prize box, friendship jar, "I caught someone doing something good when ____!")
First grade • Noise level of one group • Transitional behavior • Poor word decoding skills • Students require attention as they work in centers • Some students have low word encoding and decoding levels	• Add more visual-auditory-kinesthetic-tactile (VAKT) elements (e.g., salt trays with phonics lessons) • Wilson checklist (http://www.fundations.com/PM_info.aspx) to document current levels • Jolly Phonics (http://jollylearning.co.uk/gallery/) • Step-by-step task analysis for transitional skills when students return from electives posted on the wall and / or individualized as needed • Explore ongoing centers (e.g., artist corner, sensory area, my community) • Think about fewer, but in-depth, activities at centers and pairing students • Establish behavioral plan with student to increase appropriate behavior with alternative ways to channel energies (e.g., "When I feel the need to talk, I could do this instead"—kneaded eraser, doodle). • Continually introduce positive statements (e.g., "I will follow our rules to ____.") • Choose personal motivators in a simple chart: <table><tr><td>doodle</td><td>kneaded eraser</td></tr><tr><td>trucks</td><td>____</td></tr></table>
Second grade • Excellent co-teaching/*marriage* ☺ • Students have unique personalities with diverse academic and behavioral levels (e.g., distractibility, self-control, self-esteem)	• Classroom character lessons (e.g., "Losing Is Winning!") • Social story about what happens in a dodgeball game ☺ • Explore a class reward system • Incorporate an "I Remember" and "Enrichment Station/Corner" for students who require repetition and/or advancements • Investigate ways to add more technology and universal design for learning (UDL) elements at Center for Applied Special Technology (www.cast.org)

Co-Teachers' Communications	Inclusion Strategies/Co-Teaching Plans and Goals Discussed
• Co-teaching models explored, but room size and noise level interfere at times • Students respond to structured, nonthreatening, and positive environment • Excellent whole-part-whole configuration with transitions during science stations	• Allow scaffolding with writing frames • Offer Bare Books (http://www.barebooks.com/) as incentives • Explore ways to add more centers and parallel teaching to continually decrease teacher-student ratio • Offer perceptual activities as discussed (http://www.eyecanlearn.com/)
Third grade • Scheduling/transitioning is tough for some • Students have additional emotional needs (e.g., channeling anger) • Lesson differentiation necessary due to varying reading levels and motivation	• Explore additional co-teaching models with centers • Add more VAKT elements to meetings and activities (e.g., visual cues in behavioral charts, "Turn-Talk-Do") • Creative twists to lessons (e.g., "Reality Classroom," graph individual baseline behavior levels) • Have a behavioral chart with visual cues (e.g., task analysis—"What to do when I return from an elective," "What's next?" charts) • Thematic lessons (e.g., "Change: Butterflies, Seasons, and Me") • Survey students to develop more self-regulation and awareness (e.g., "Things That Are Difficult for Me")

Fourth grade
• Some students require additional sensitivities about differences
• Great organization and structure with routines and transitions
• Adult circulation and attention given to students keep students on task and offer immediate feedback
• Diversified activities engage students across the curriculum
• Students need additional keyboarding programs/skills
• Love the modeling, animated storytelling, and great room rapport with the students interacting with each other and teachers
• Students engaged and enthusiastic about learning
	• Explore additional co-teaching models with planners to:
	  ○ Lower teacher-student ratio
	  ○ Define co-teaching roles during lessons
	  ○ Differentiate lessons with baseline, advancing, and more challenging objectives for whole classes, small groups, and individual students
	• Offer keyboarding practice (http://www.learninggamesforkids.com/keyboarding_games/typing-course.html)
	• disABILITY awareness (e.g., "Shake It Up" from *Embracing disABILITIES*—Karten, 2008a)
	• Bibliotherapy booklist
	• Introduce more structured stations; with activities that offer repetition, remediation, and enrichment (e.g., social studies with multiple intelligence menus, math word problems for mixed grouping, classroom/school newspaper)
	• Infuse more VAKT elements in lessons (e.g., tack a picture of the keyboard above student laptops, more student movement in morning meetings with associated visuals that describe abstract themes, examples/nonexamples—e.g., homelessness, respect)
	  • Allow some students to sort, classify, or match pictures

Fifth grade • Attention and focusing issues, with some students needing frequent reminders to stay on task • Classroom space not conducive to varying co-teaching models • Students' academic levels of independence vary	• Include other co-teaching models as appropriate • Explore lesson plan book and online resources to document accommodations and levels of participation ("Hierarchy of Skills") • Divide lessons with baseline, more advanced, and challenging assignments • Infuse into different stations spelling/word work three to four times a week and then branch out to other subjects • Tap into individual student strengths • Encourage student interactions with structured cooperative stations and assigned student roles, research/artist's corner

(Continued)

Figure 8.3 (Continued)

Co-Teachers' Communications	Inclusion Strategies/Co-Teaching Plans and Goals Discussed
• Co-teachers share and divide class during book clubs with parallel teaching, small groups, and often team teaching • Great higher-order thinking skills imbued with place value symbols • Good auditory cues and reminders (e.g., "Give yourself a chance to think before you talk," "All eyes forward," "Voices off!") • All students were actively involved with money manipulatives and enthusiastic about math	• Enlist peer mentors as appropriate • Add more VAKT elements with one-to-one student in math lesson (e.g., 200s chart, TouchMath) • Explore functional math skills • Include student in whole-class lessons within the classroom with positive contributions on different level (e.g., modified worksheet with less complexity), or sequence, identify, or sort numbers with 10s columns instead of more complex problems, manipulate base 10 blocks • Develop more self-regulated and attentive learners with "Eyes On/Mind On" program • Incorporate kinesthetic "brain breaks" • Introduce motivators such as earning "What I Like Time" as a reward

Sixth grade
• Working as a team with lead-assist, parallel, small groups, and one-to-one as needed
• Whole-class writing lesson with lead-assist and small writing groups
• Incredible VAKT elements with *Beowulf* pictures and other auditory and visual cues for academics, organization, and behavior (e.g., "Put your listening ears on!" history timeline)
• Excellent atmosphere and student connections
• Concentrated on the big picture
	• Explore additional lesson planning forms and online documents
	• Offer students additional writing tools (e.g., transitional, sensory word lists)
	• Continue to encourage higher-order thinking skills in lessons
	• Mention the "heart of what I am teaching you"—perhaps students can have their own heart lists, too!
	• Share additional visuals/graphic organizers from these sites:
	  o Pics4learning: http://pics.tech4learning.com/
	  o Kidspiration: http://www.inspiration.com/Kidspiration/examples
	  o Freeology: http://freeology.com/

Art • Students actively engaged in creating meaningful mandalas • What a truly collaborative and meaningful project • Connected to the students as each one contributed his or her mandala and message to the frame • Structure in place and classroom atmosphere • Saw a snapshot of a given day with a given class, gave suggestions via e-mail since the teachers were preparing for Friday event	• Teacher-friendly "Interdisciplinary Planner" shared with colleagues as encouragement and reminder to communicate upcoming lessons (e.g., students can draw a curriculum picture of multiplication, symmetry, science experiment, character/scene in book they just read, historical figure/setting, respectful communities, individuals helping others) • This link offers a math connection: www.coolmath.com • Jigsaw and investigate artists by having students emulate their favorite artist's style and create their own interpretation to present to the class. This would work from Paul Klee to Matisse, Jacob Lawrence, and more. • If you are not familiar with this series by the MOMA (Philip Yenawine), it has themes that help students with visual perceptual skills identify colors, lines, shapes, and stories • For those who finish ahead of others, have ongoing art projects/centers (e.g., scaling/gridding pictures, art journals, sketching corner, media exploration) • VSA (www.vsarts.org) is an incredible site for exploring and perhaps collaborating with • Bare Books encourages students to create their own picture books and puzzles • Tim Kelly is the artist who has the autism puzzle project. He collaborates with different schools, so perhaps . . .
Music • Create new and relevant rubrics to meaningfully assess the arts—especially through an inclusion lens	• Collaborative curriculum planning • Art and music games: http://www.learninggamesforkids.com/art_and_music_games.html • Educational songs: http://www.learninggamesforkids.com/preschool_kindergarten_videos.html • Explore music rubrics at http://www.rubrics4teachers.com/music.php

The inclusion coaching communications and recommendations shown in Figure 8.4 resulted from grade-level meetings with middle school teachers.

Figure 8.4   Middle School Team Meetings

Communications	Action Plan and Recommendations
Grade 5 • Co-teaching relationships are working well (e.g., sharing expertise and responsibilities) • Flexibility within inclusion structure • Support/resource model offered students extra help with organization and remediation • Challenges exist when classroom numbers are too large—prefer students spread out over clusters (recommended parallel/team teaching, small focus groups to lower ratio) **Grade 6** • Spoke about assessment choices to establish baseline levels (e.g., language arts, math such as http://www.testdesigner.com/questions) • Important to indicate student gains as well as proficiency to note the progress achieved, even if the student does not receive a high or passing grade (e.g., communicate gains to students and families) • Varying co-teaching models and responsibilities dependent upon students and subjects • Want heterogeneous grouping within classes, not only basic skills instruction and special education • Exploring resources **Grade 7** • Discussion of placing co-teachers in addition to teacher assistants in social studies and science (e.g., content knowledge, scheduling, sharing responsibilities—teacher assistants often pulled in different directions) • Scheduling one grade level per special education teacher • Additional co-planning times • Differing student levels with academics and behavior	• Map quarterly lessons with an overview of objectives that outline the big ideas for each quarter. Add Common Core State Standards (CCSS) numbers and then share all with class in student-friendly language—examples of quarterly mapping shared across the curriculum in science, social studies, and algebra (CCSS iPad app available from http://itunes.apple.com/us/app/common-core-standards/id439424555?mt=8) • Include study and social skill objectives, along with academic ones, in lesson/unit planners throughout the year • Give packet to each teacher with student surveys • Establish a structured system with response to intervention (RTI) in place and reviewed at team meetings/co-planning sessions every four to six weeks (twice each marking period) for whole classes, small groups, individual students • Vary co-teaching models—thinking about how to use stations, team teach, apply a parallel lesson (e.g., half the class works with one teacher to show a ratio as a decimal, while the other half expresses the ratio as a fraction; then either teachers or students switch groups); always allow opportunities for both teachers to share responsibilities from the planning to instructional and assessment decisions • Set up an ongoing structured system of groups within the classroom (instead of pullout). Recommend 10–12 minutes twice a week for review, on-level, and challenging assignments with smaller groups of students—sending a strong communication for students to be prepared and not wait for the day before the test to ask questions and gain clarification, which circumvents misconceptions escalating. This ongoing classroom setup communicates the importance of review for all students and offers the students with individualized education plans more in-class support without being singled out • Continue to incorporate kinesthetic elements (e.g., role play as animals who detect an upcoming earthquake) • Capitalize on each teacher's strengths and continue feedback with ongoing communications; face-to-face at team meetings, interactive co-teaching planners e-mailed with collaborative input • Establish baseline level of student performance and levels beyond the AIMS testing (e.g., curriculum-based ones, writing samples, student task analysis of behavior, functional-ecological assessment, study skills checklist reviewed and documented with concrete evidence—student work samples)

(Continued)

Figure 8.4   (Continued)

Communications	Action Plan and Recommendations
Grade 8 • Physical space within the classroom to offer assistance without pulling out students across the hall • Important to bridge the gap from year to year (e.g., observe next year's students in current classrooms, teacher communication) • Subject-specific assignments vs. following students—pros and cons discussed	• Offer students more metacognition about their levels and the curriculum objectives for each unit (e.g., amount of seconds they were on task—followed directions/participated in class discussion each period (a co-teacher or teaching assistant can record data) • Explore more about universal design for learning (UDL) at http://www.cast.org/. Students can create their own book at Book Builder (http://bookbuilder.cast.org/). Check out this video for an overview of UDL principles: http://www.udlcenter.org/resource_library/videos/udlcenter/udl. • Continue the collaboration with each other (interdisciplinary lessons when possible, common academic vocabulary) • Investigate the books and online resources for teachers and students along with web resources about specific disabilities to plan, instruct, document . . . • Encourage teams of teachers to form professional learning community book clubs • E-mail to continue the collaboration!
	A packet of resources with teacher planners and documentation was shared with team leaders and groups for both educator and student use.

The next planning chart, Figure 8.5, offers staff an opportunity to reflect upon the inclusion factors.

 Figure 8.5   Inclusion Coaching Planning Sheet: My/Our Thoughts About . . .

Trying Different Interventions and/or Co-teaching Models	Pacing Lessons/Curriculum Mapping
Varying Classroom Structures: • Whole class • Small groups • One-to-one • Cooperative learning stations	Differentiating Objectives, Instruction, Assessments
Applying the 18 Inclusion Principles	Other

9

Inclusion Lenses

ATTITUDES

Helen Keller poignantly stated: "Optimism is the faith that leads to achievement; nothing can be done without hope and confidence" (Keller, 1903, p. 67).
Her keen insights can be applied to inclusion school settings. If teachers believe
that students are capable of achieving continued successes, then lessons are
designed with appropriate and differentiated strategies that allow these achievements to happen. If educators are coached to highlight and recognize that they
possess the competencies to make inclusion successes happen, then the learning is enhanced for all. If administrators and educators believe the obverse to be
true, then pessimistic attitudes permeate to students. Since there is no template
for inclusion or a definition of *a typical inclusion child,* acceptances of inclusion
will vary, but attitudinal reflections are crucial for all.

> Attitudinal barriers were a recurring theme in data. It is clear that
> inclusion will remain a significant challenge if practitioners are not
> committed to its principles and it will be impossible if practitioners fail
> to embrace their responsibility for the education of all children.
> (Glazzard, 2011, p. 56)

School leaders who coach teachers need to understand change to address
resistance (Knight, 2009). Neuroscientists speak about creating new circuits
with increased attention or awareness on something new, reflections that acti-
vate different parts of the brain, and insights that lead to immediate actions to
achieve results (Rock & Schwartz, 2006). Administrators, educators, and
school staff at times face challenges that often fall under the *TTWWADI* (that's
the way we always did it) *syndrome* umbrella. It is OK to repeat prior successful
practices, as long as innovative ideas are also welcomed and applied. Research
denotes that changes to inclusion classroom routines and practices are essential. Educators who are delivering lessons at the same pace will not reach some

students with disabilities (King-Sears, 2008). Instructional accommodations and adaptations are never generic and may be applicable to some learners but not all students (Paterson, 2007). If differences are acknowledged and accepted, then the appropriate planning highlights student strengths with lessons that increase learning. Frustrations that exist for students, families, staff, and administration are often part of the inclusion process. The number of work hours and students present also influence attitudes (Gal, Schreur, & Engel-Yeger, 2010). However, administrators who support appropriate staff development loudly state that inclusion learning communities need additional coaching supports. Before any program begins, there must be not only staff *buy-in* but also ongoing belief that collaborative, structured, reflective, compassionate, and professional attitudes will make inclusion work well in each and every environment.

Administrators and coaches who seek input from their staff and value what their educators view as crucial topics take many steps forward that allow staff to adopt and implement effective research-based practices in their inclusion classrooms. This crucial and sometimes overlooked step is the precursor that treats teachers as professional collaborators instead of as recipients of directives that they might feign accepting.

It is also critical for everyone to have a positive attitude about disabilities. Figure 9.1 offers some cross-curricular critical thinking skills for professionals. It is intended to generate discussion and to confront and remove attitudinal barriers.

INCLUSION AND CO-TEACHING WISH LIST

School leaders need to always know the pulse of their general education and special education staff. The following summarizes an *inclusion wish list* that was generated during professional development (PD) coaching sessions with elementary, middle school, and high school teachers. Not every concern is a feasible one, due to practicalities such as budget concerns and staff dynamics, but acknowledging each of them is essential. This list was later shared with school building administrators who were at the planning stages for the next year's inclusion programs and co-teaching assignments.

1. Smaller student-teacher ratio with lower percentage of students with special education needs in an inclusion class (e.g., not stacking the class with students with behavioral issues and English learners, in addition to students with IEPs)

2. More common planning time with prep periods (e.g., two weekly team planning meetings)

3. More PD on how to implement co-teaching models

4. Replace some staff or department meetings with time to meet with co-teachers

5. Time for co-teachers to review IEPs prior to the start of the school year

6. Work with the same teacher from year to year to establish consistent partnerships

Figure 9.1 Disability-Curriculum Analogies

Read these similes and metaphors, and then independently or collectively write additional ones for each of the content areas.		
Subject	*Metaphor*	*Simile*
Math	A disability is a decimal that is sometimes regarded by others as less worthy than a whole number.	A disability is like a decimal, seeking the same *points* in life.
Science	A disability is a telescope trying to grasp shining stars.	A disability is sometimes like a microscopic slide that has its traits magnified for others to view.
Social Studies	A disability is often a map without a legend.	A disability is like a map that represents more than what is seen.
Reading	A disability is a book that reveals itself, page by page.	A disability is as varied as the genres in a library.
Writing	A disability is an epic poem.	A disability is like a novel, revealing its plot.
Languages	A disability is a story that sometimes requires subtitles for others to understand.	A disability is as beautiful as a romance language.
Art/Music	A disability is a picture with elements in the foreground and background.	A disability is as joyous and as talent-filled as a Broadway musical!

Source: Adapted from Karten, T. (2008a). *Embracing disABILITIES in the classroom: Strategies to maximize students' assets.* Thousand Oaks, CA: Corwin

7. Have input on co-teaching partnerships

8. More in-class support classes and sections

9. Real support, not lip service

10. Trust-filled environment between administrators and educators—not *us vs. them* atmosphere

11. More professional training for new social studies and science curriculum

12. Laptops and mini notebooks available to classrooms with better technology (e.g., Kindle, Bookshare, Inspiration, and more individualization)

13. Education for the school and parent community with regard to the benefits of the co-teaching classroom so it is not viewed as the special education classroom

14. Ongoing training to assess what is working and what can be improved

15. Establish measurable criteria to decide whether students should move into an inclusion class or remain in a resource room setting

16. Building-based administrators to observe co-teaching classrooms and directly work with teachers to improve the program, not team members who try to solve problems but are not decision makers

17. Educate administrators on the value of an inclusion classroom and why co-taught students are placed there (e.g., it is not a behavioral class)

18. A chance for co-teachers and administrators to meet together to share ideas and concerns beyond an August training

19. Class lists for co-teaching classes are shared early on

20. Inform teachers at the end of the year about next year's co-teaching program to allow planning time

21. More information about specific disabilities (e.g., dyscalculia, autism)

EDUCATOR STRENGTHS

Teachers are often advised to instruct learners through strength paradigms rather than focusing on students' weaker areas. It is also essential that professional learning experiences tap into the expertise and collective knowledge of all staff (Killion & Hirsh, 2012). Just as students in inclusive classrooms cannot be coached to learn by using a one-size-fits-all approach, all educators cannot be treated the same way, since teachers are at various career and performance levels, with unique subject knowledge, strengths, and interests.

Suppose a teacher loves music and taps into that strength by sharing curriculum lyrics with students and has his or her students create their own songs as well. The obverse is also true. If students do not respond well to musical-rhythmic presentations, then they may need more logical or verbal-linguistic presentations, even if that is not an educator's strength. At times inclusion coaches capitalize on educators' strengths and ask them to share their expertise with colleagues. For instance, if co-teachers have mastered parallel teaching, they share their strategies with other educators by inviting them into their classrooms. Administrators such as building principals, assistant principals, and supervisors offer classroom coverage to encourage this type of ongoing collegial sharing.

When an educator acknowledges his or her weaker area, it becomes a stronger one, since this reflection allows a teacher to improve upon his or her skills. Admitting that there is always something new to learn stops stagnation and allows an educator to grow and learn. This knowledge is then shared with students. This range may include, but is not limited to, researching more about a certain disability, learning a new instructional math strategy, enhancing classroom management skills, and perhaps finding out how to create an Animoto slide show (information can be accessed from Animoto Productions, 2013). Having well-thought-out objectives and lesson plans that connect with students on their levels means that educators have their own plans for professional growth to connect to their own levels.

Other factors, such as patience, flexibility, organization, professionalism, and structure, help educators figure out ways that the students within their classrooms will gain the knowledge and skills across the curriculum. Addressing the needs of diverse learners requires much knowledge but also a great deal of perseverance, enthusiasm, and dedication to the profession. Educator strengths also include excellent communication and collaborative skills with administrators, colleagues, students, families, and community organizations. It is important to agree that you will not always agree but at the same time be coached to have open channels with all inclusive stakeholders.

Another crucial educator strength is to instill motivation in students. Educators require excellent knowledge of their content areas, but they also need more knowledge on how to communicate with and motivate students. Passionate teachers usually find ways to connect to everyone. Overall, educator strengths are sharpened over time with more experience and supportive leaders.

10

Taking the Inclusion Walk

Instruction, Data, and Assessments

Student, family, staff, administrative, legislative, and curricular needs, demands, and supports shape the rules and roles of each inclusion community. Questions that are collaboratively asked, researched, explored, and discussed define the focus of the collaborative teams. Student levels must be determined to honor academic, social, emotional, behavioral, communication, study skills, and functional objectives and goals. Input is required from administrators, teachers, coaches, students, families, related staff, and all team members. Collecting and organizing the data with accurate information from standardized tests, informal instructional assessments, observations, student profiles, interviews, focus groups, opinion surveys, classroom-based evidence, Section 504 accommodation plans, IEP narratives, and more is critical. When students with different ability levels and skills are educated in the same classroom, that classroom needs to provide appropriate scaffolding and accommodations that offer both remediation and enrichment.

The *inclusion walk* involves examining data and honoring assessment options. The data may also be nonacademic, such as a breakdown of demographics, disciplinary procedures, attendance records, PD opportunities, and graduation rates (Holcomb, 2012), to determine and discuss patterns and decide on actions. Once information is gathered, conversations, surveys, and focus groups collaboratively review the issues that factor into inclusion decisions. Assessments can be standardized, curriculum based, or individually driven. Instructionally based assessments can range from chapter tests to quizzes, exit cards, homework checks, lab reports, writing samples, math drills, oral readings, speeches, debates, cloze exercises, checklists, rating scales, observations, and more. Assessments are not exclusively designed to reveal test grades that teachers average into a quarterly letter grade that is placed on a report card. Curriculum-based monitoring more importantly measures student performance and in turn guides instruction and coaching recommendations. Both formal and informal assessments are given to determine reading fluency, comprehension, writing skills, math competencies, spelling acumen, and other academic, social, perceptual, and visual-motor skills (Wright, n.d.). Progress is graphed, recorded, and examined by professionals who collaboratively review the effectiveness of interventions. Educators then record students' progress, mastery, or difficulties so that they can decide on further appropriate strategies and interventions.

Inclusion coaches, educators, and leaders use assessments to preview student skills, determine progression, record mastery, and adjust programs. As appropriate, assessments include information that reveals psychoeducational levels and achievements, curriculum mastery, personality screenings, social needs, visual-motor skills, memory levels, visual-spatial skills, executive functioning, phonological awareness, and more. Examples include, but are not limited to, those developed by Woodcock-Johnson, Weschler, Kaufman, Peabody, KeyMath, Brigance, and AIMSweb. These assessments may be criterion or norm referenced, respectively, referring to performances on intended goals and objectives or in comparison to other students. Since the Partnership for Assessment of Readiness for College and Careers (PARCC) and the Smarter Balanced Assessment Consortium (SBAC) are designing online assessments for the Common Core State Standards, instruction needs to include technological components as well. Inclusive stakeholders can review the following sites to gain further assessment insights.

Assessment Insights

- Office of Special Education: http://www.osepideasthatwork.org/toolkit/index. asp, http://www.osepideasthatwork.org/parentkit/AltAssessFAQ.asp

- National Dissemination Center for Children with Disabilities Accommodations in Assessment: http://nichcy.org/schoolage/iep/iepcontents/assessment

- University of Georgia Disability Resource Center: http://drc.uga.edu/ disabilities/suggestedmeasures.php

- Curriculum Associates: http://www.curriculumassociates.com/products/detail .asp?title=BrigCIBS

- Test Designer: http://www.testdesigner.com/questions

- Cool Tools: Project Central: http://www.paec.org/itrk3/files/pdfs/readingpdfs/ cooltoolsall.pdf

- Partnership for Assessment of Readiness for College and Careers: http:// www.parcconline.org

- Smarter Balanced Assessment Consortium: http://www.smarterbalanced.org

---

When principals, team leaders, and coaches have data discussions with educators, it is important to discuss assessment factors that influence the final grade received. As examples, encourage educators to offer valid assessments with wording on written tests that is jargon-free but focused on the skills. Salend (2012) suggests that teachers share strategies that help students deal with possible stress. These strategies include imagery and relaxation techniques. Offering students ideas on how to study and be better test takers is also crucial. This includes teaching students how to develop study guides and lists of possible questions, review games, evaluate notes and readings, develop collaborative peer study groups, and know the difference between good and better answers on multiple-choice tests, what an excellent essay response looks like as opposed to a fair one, what the words *most likely* or *least likely* refer to, and what it means to show your work when solving a math problem.

Inclusion rules with structured intervention plans, beginning from the planning to the instructional and assessment stages. Core curriculum standards must be aligned and transferred to classroom inclusion standards of good teaching practices. Inclusion standards involve interventions that value the data and how students learn best. Brain-based learning, multisensory instruction, multiple intelligences, cooperative learning, targeting learning styles, reducing stress, and valuing self-reflections, along with the 18 inclusion principles mentioned in Part I, are infused into lessons. There are research-based practices that teachers can use to organize their instruction and improve students' memory and understanding. This includes providing examples with practice, spacing learning over time, developing abstract-concrete connections, valuing multiple representations, and incorporating higher-order thinking skills in lessons (Scruggs, Mastropieri, Berkeley, & Graetz, 2010). Students need learning opportunities to sharpen their critical thinking skills through challenging activities that develop increased literacy, numeracy, and cross-disciplinary skills. When all students are afforded the opportunities to simultaneously benefit from the inclusive environment, then it is truly an inclusive one.

The professionals need to first decide what is *appropriate* for each inclusion community by taking an *inclusion walk* to identify the data, instruction, and assessments. Coaches and school leaders help by honoring the characteristics, experiences, skills, strengths, attitudes, and levels of the students, families, educators, and collaborative staff in each learning environment.

APPRAISING THE INCLUSION GAPS AND AMBIGUITIES

Under federal law—Public Law 108-446, the Individuals with Disabilities Education Act (IDEA 2004)—the *regular classroom,* or *general education classroom,* is considered to be the least restrictive environment (LRE) on the continuum of services for a child with special needs. This has been mandated since the Education for All Handicapped Children Act (Public Law 94-142) back in the 1970s. The general education placement allows a student to be educated with peers who are not disabled, to the maximum extent appropriate. Alternative placement options are delineated on the LRE continuum if it is determined that the general education classroom is not the appropriate environment to service an individual child's needs. The legislation further discusses terms such as the *nature* or *severity of the disability* and whether the education can satisfactorily occur in *regular* classes with the use of *supplementary aids and services.*

Full inclusion allows students to receive their instruction and services within the general education setting. Accommodations and modifications are outlined, along with considerations of what meaningful participation constitutes. Parents and families have procedural safeguards and specific due process rights. Educators, related staff, teams, and families plan an IEP for each student, and the progress is reported to parents at set intervals during the school year. Consideration is given to transition services that help prepare the student for future placements and decisions, along with an extended school year (ESY) program if it is deemed appropriate to maintain learning gains. Even with a written IEP in place, there are inclusion ambiguities and gaps.

There is at times a lack of agreement among home and school environments concerning students' LREs, inclusion placements, programs, and services during the planning stages and beyond. This includes differences in attitudes, actions, and experiences from families of students with and without disabilities, classroom peers, educators, related staff, and administrators. One principal vocalized concerns over the effect that a student with serious emotional disturbance has on an inclusion classroom (Oluwole, 2009). Some community members embrace inclusion, while other community members have prejudicial attitudes, anxieties, and oppositions (Crowson & Brandes, 2010). Another study examined whether the amount of contact with minority and majority groups reduces prejudice or whether the inverse is true, that prejudice reduces contact (Binder et al., 2009). At times there are gaps between beliefs and practices, as is denoted by professionals in an inclusive program for young children who were uncertain about how to implement IEPs or specific inclusion strategies—for example, applicable strategies for a student with motor or communication impairments (Bruns & Mogharreban, 2007). As this study denotes, educators are often willing, but at times ill trained or inexperienced or otherwise unqualified, to choose and/or deliver inclusion interventions.

Barriers confront special educators in learning communities (Griffin, Kilgore, Winn, & Otis-Willborn, 2008; Kozik, Cooney, Vinciguerra, Grade, & Black, 2009). This includes issues with caseloads, job descriptions, and scheduling. Educators need to learn how to differentiate instruction and assessments (Braden, Shroder, & Buckley, 2001). Inclusion in middle schools and high schools is complicated by gaps in skill levels and scheduling challenges (Kozik, Cooney, Vinciguerra, Gradel, & Black, 2009). As research denotes, inclusion attitudes vary from individuals who are unsure of what their inclusion role is or even doubt inclusion effectiveness to individuals who embrace and applaud inclusion. However, ambiguities allow professionals to share multiple perspectives to personalize, construct, and strengthen their beliefs and decisions about inclusion programs and practices. Just as a classroom is heterogeneous, so is inclusion coaching. Overall, gaps and ambiguities are decreased when compassion, awareness, professionalism, structures, and reflections prevail.

PART IV

Professional Development

11

Framing Inclusion

BASIC STRUCTURES

Professional development opportunities need to be highly structured to foster productive and respectful inclusive relationships with all educators and supportive staff. The days of "We will have a one-day inservice to teach you everything you need to know, and then you can go do it" are gone! Collaborative yearlong programs are required to ensure that inclusion lives and breathes within healthy supportive schools. Aside from focusing on teaching students with special needs, inclusion professional development (PD) needs to be aligned with district goals. Inclusion PD sessions initiate and monitor programs with quality instruction, supports, and services that foster student achievements and school visions.

Principals, school leaders, and coaches need to allot weekly and, if possible, daily common planning time for educators to formulate plans to raise students' achievements across the content areas. In addition, school leaders who allow educators input to share responsibilities from planning stages to facilitating meetings are then significantly promoting professional development. Some general and special educators will need additional guidance before they can independently guide others. Acceptable models and rubrics are sometimes formulated and shared with outside consultants who help guide the staff to enhance their professional development. Then, educators are encouraged to expand upon the learning to take ownership of the professional learning experiences. Based upon collective experiences, everyone's participation is valued.

Enhancing Professional Practice: A Framework for Teaching (Danielson, 2007) outlines four domains of teaching responsibility as planning and preparation, classroom environment, instruction, and professional responsibilities. This includes but is not limited to knowledge of students, setting instructional outcomes, managing classroom procedures, being flexible and responsive to students and families, and reflecting and growing as a professional. Inclusion classrooms have their own domains, as shown in Figure 11.1.

Figure 11.1 Inclusion Frameworks

Inclusion Foundation	Inclusive Environment
Being prepared with planned and appropriate lessons, materials, resources, supports, and instructional strategies for diverse learners	Creating a safe, nonjudgmental, accepting environment that values differences and high expectations for all learners
Inclusive Collaborative Practices	*Professional Inclusion*
Respectfully collaborating and communicating with grade-level teams, coaches, co-teachers, administrators, and students to deliver differentiated instructional practices that honor students' levels and potentials	Believing that teaching and learning are interrelated, ongoing, and nonnegotiable to advance the skills of all learners within inclusive classrooms by consistently reflecting on growth

Invite educators to collaboratively design their own frameworks, using a form such as Figure 11.2.

Figure 11.2 Our Inclusion Framework

Inclusion Foundation	Inclusive Environment
Being prepared with . . .	Creating . . .
Inclusive Collaborative Practices	*Professional Inclusion*
Respectfully collaborating and communicating . . .	Believing that teaching and learning are. . . .

CEC EDUCATOR PREPARATION STANDARDS

The Council for Exceptional Children (CEC, 2013a) delineates seven preparation standards with elements that identify the knowledge and skills for initial-level special educators (Figure 11.3) and advanced special education specialists (Figure 11.4). Together inclusion coaches and educators can review, synthesize, and apply the following salient points to increase their baseline knowledge of the standards to ensure that students with exceptionalities are offered the best practices so that they can develop as learners. The CEC ethical principles and practice standards offer professional competences that include maintaining challenging expectations for students with exceptionalities and infusing evidence-based and culturally responsive learning environments into both teaching and assessments. Professional development is a nonnegotiable ongoing process for special education professionals who are at all career levels. School leaders, paraeducators, parents, families, and case managers are also included. The CEC intends that research be used in accurate ways that improve the learning outcomes of students with exceptionalities. School leaders and coaches can jigsaw these professional points with staff throughout the year at monthly and weekly meetings. The exact language of the CEC standards for professional preparation and specialty sets can be accessed online (see CEC, 2013b).

Figure 11.3 Council for Exceptional Children: Initial-Level Special Education Preparation Standards (Beginning Special Education Professionals)

Standard 1—Learner Development and Individual Learning Differences (includes providing meaningful and challenging experiences for students with exceptionalities with an understanding of the influences of language, culture, and family background and how to respect individual differences)
Standard 2—Learning Environments (includes educational implications of exceptionalities; family, cultural, and environmental impacts along with the consideration of emotional well-being, social interactions, and self-determination)
Standard 3—Curricular Content Knowledge (includes the development of general and specialized curricula across content areas)

(Continued)

Figure 11.3 (Continued)

Standard 4—Assessment (involves the usage of formal and informal assessments to correctly guide educational decisions)
Standard 5—Instructional Planning and Strategies (involves evidence-based instructional strategies with a consideration of individual exceptionalities, transitions, communications, families, cultures, and behaviors)
Standard 6—Professional Learning and Ethical Practice (engaging in lifelong learning to advance the profession, including advocacy and mentoring)
Standard 7—Collaboration (includes respectful communication with other professionals, students, and families)
Inclusion Team Members:

After review of the initial CEC standards, collaborative inclusion teams are invited to peruse Figure 11.4, which has advanced preparation standards for special education specialists to continually record how the standards are applied in their professional communities to ensure that the knowledge and skills to assist learners with exceptionalities are continuously advanced.

Figure 11.4 CEC Special Education Specialist Advanced Preparation Standards

Standard 1—Assessment (valid and reliable assessments, bias minimized, evaluation of the effectiveness of both programs and practices, decision making with screening, eligibility, and IEP goals)
Standard 2—Curricular Content Knowledge (alignment of challenging and meaningful curriculum and content for students with exceptional needs, with the selection, development, and implementation of comprehensive curricula that include general and specialized academic content and effective teaching strategies)
Standard 3—Programs, Services, and Outcomes (appropriate implementation of evidence-based practices, relevant legislation, and assistive technology with an understanding of social, cultural, and economic diversity, and individual learner differences)
Standard 4—Research and Inquiry (instructional improvements that are based on the engagement of research and inquiry to identify and improve practices and interventions)
Standard 5—Leadership and Policy (goals and effective policies, ethical, linguistically, and culturally respectful practices, collegial and productive work environments, and appropriate resources to support learners with exceptionalities)
Standard 6—Professional and Ethical Practice (planning and engagement in lifelong learning and professional practices at all organizational levels)
Standard 7—Collaboration (increase of collaborative skills to advance programs and services, resolve conflicts, and improve outcomes for individuals with exceptionalities and their families)
Inclusion Team Members:

Professional development that is standards based connects learning with student results. Learning Forward (2011), an international association of learning educators, declares that standards-based professional learning is the catalyst that changes educator knowledge, skills, and dispositions, which in turn influences educator practice and student results. This professional development is essential for educators of students with and without exceptionalities. The diversity that exists in today's classroom demands a diverse set of professional skills, with educators continually refining their practices. Within this past decade, the increasing number of students who are educated within inclusive environments drive administrators, general and special educators, and all related staff to seek out more knowledge about exceptional learners and research-based inclusive practices. The Common Core State Standards (CCSS) are applicable for all groups of learners, with inclusive educators holding high learning expectations for all of their students. It is not debatable whether students can learn, but the question is often what professional coaching is required to ensure that the optimum practices are in place in that inclusive classroom.

RESEARCHING DISABILITIES

Inclusion rules with increased awareness and compassion. Students have differing abilities, not disabilities. Viewing students through this strength paradigm values a positive mind-set that says, "How can I teach this student?" as opposed to "Can I teach this student?" Deleting the prefix *im-* from the adjective *impossible* says that inclusion is attainable. Therefore, within each student's labeled *disability* is the base word *ability*. It is also important to remember that students who share a classification label are individuals, not clones of each other. Disability groups are heterogeneous, yet researching specific differences assists educators in their quest to discover the strategies and interventions that highlight students' stronger modalities and strengths. You can also learn *from,* instead of exclusively *about,* students. Knowing the characteristics students with certain disabilities are apt to display opens many *inclusion doors,* yielding worthwhile instructional decisions.

Inclusion learning communities collaboratively determine the populations of students, strategies, and interventions to be researched. Together educators and all staff members sift through, critique, and appropriately apply the research to specific classroom environments, school communities, administrators, co-teachers, related staff, and students. This foundation of knowledge allows everyone to collectively plan proactive supportive inclusion decisions. The element of surprise generated from each student can never be deleted, but professional knowledge is invaluable. This often involves the examination and sharing of past and current performances and inclusion experiences, along with discussions and conferences with students, former teachers, and family members to match the interventions with student data.

Information is often just a *click away.* These screenshots and online sites reveal just a glimpse into the available disability research. It is mind-boggling how quickly information is available. The toughest part is sifting through the quantity of disability sites to then focus on quality information about dis-ABILITIES. The next screenshot indicates the tens of millions of sites obtained within a fraction of a second for the word *disabilities*.

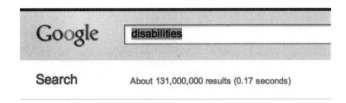

This screenshot was accessed with a Google search on March 15, 2012. The screenshots that follow display visual representations of topics related to disabilities and were obtained by using the former Wonder Wheel feature of Google with the word *disabilities* chosen as the hub.

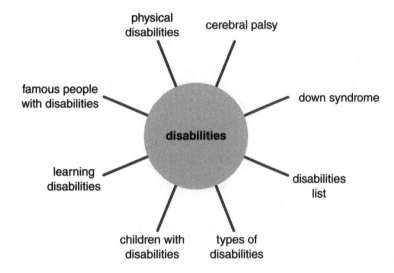

Clicking on one of the spokes, *learning disabilities* yielded this result.

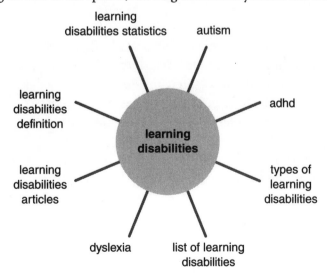

The search is refined even further by clicking on the word *dyslexia*.

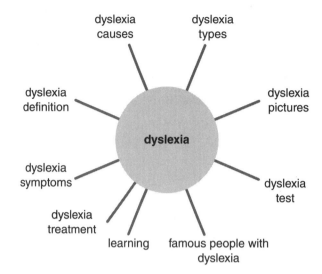

Investigating the spoke titled *definition of dyslexia* yielded this result.

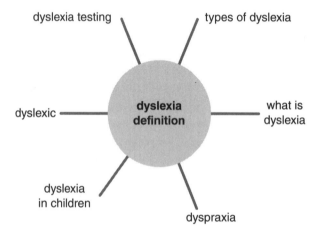

Afterward, the results are narrowed down further to a particular topic or subtopic that team members, grade levels, and/or co-teachers concentrate on. Inclusion coaches assist educators in compiling a list of disabilities to research and jigsaw, based on educator prior knowledge, needs, interests, and classroom dynamics. After critical research of the information available, the findings on various differences are presented to other staff and family members, using instructional deliveries and presentations that honor visual, auditory, and kinesthetic modalities, multiple intelligences, and learning styles. For example, one group presents the information in a song about autism, while another group creates a WebQuest that focuses on attention deficit/hyperactivity disorder (ADHD) or dyscalculia, as another group of professionals explores students with hearing impairments or intellectual disabilities by designing a Prezi. Professionals generate a collage that highlights information about strategies and characteristics of students who are twice-exceptional or role-play the effectiveness of behavioral intervention plans and how students with more severe emotional differences are prepared to leave interim alternative educational settings to enter inclusive settings. The ultimate goal is to collaboratively increase individual and collective knowledge about students' abilities and to match inclusion strategies with appropriate instructional classroom decisions. A consummate professional is then intertwined with the inclusion knowledge and research that match each inclusion environment.

Inclusive resources *include* coaches, student support teams, families, fiction and nonfiction books, problem-based learning activities, critical thinking skills, journals, online search engines, agencies, organizations, professional networking learning groups, blogs, and more. Innumerable sources offer educators incredible opportunities to enhance their teaching styles, gain curriculum knowledge, hone disability awareness, foster positive classroom peer relationships, improve student outcomes, and network with other professionals.

This collaborative sharing allows administrators, educators, and families the ability to apply appropriate inclusion interventions to individual students, small groups, and whole classes. Planning for successes allows professional communities to widen their background knowledge to collaboratively refine and bounce inclusion insights off one another. The intention is for general and special education philosophies to become blended, offering students and educators opportunities to expand and apply the knowledge gained to inclusive classrooms. Inclusion school successes ultimately prepare individuals for more achievements as they transition outside of the classroom into life choices. In addition to the extensive resources in the bibliography, the following offers online resources and professional organizations for staff to explore to ensure and support inclusion.

Figure 11.5   Online Resources and Professional Organizations

- Council for Exceptional Children: http://www.cec.sped.org
- CAST Universal Design for Learning: http://www.cast.org/index.html
- Dr. Mac's Behavior Management Site: http://www.behavioradvisor.com
- Education Week: Teacher Blogs: http://www.edweek.org/tm/section/blogs
- Inclusion Education Services: http://inclusionworkshops.com
- Inclusion Research Institute: http://www.inclusionresearch.org/Organizations.html
- Intervention Central: http://www.interventioncentral.org
- National Dissemination Center for Children with Disabilities: http://nichcy.org
- OSEP: Ideas That Work: http://www.osepideasthatwork.org/toolkit/index.asp
- Teach All Kids: http://www.teachallkids.com
- Teaching Tolerance: http://www.tolerance.org
- What Works Clearinghouse: http://ies.ed.gov/ncee/wwc
- Wright's Law: Special Education and Advocacy: http://www.wrightslaw.com

Figure 11.6 highlights recommended sites for learning more about different populations of students within an inclusive classroom. Knowing the learning, emotional, social, behavioral, physical perceptual, communicative, and sensory needs that are presented offers appropriate accommodations for different individuals and groups of learners. Professionals are invited to relate these questions to inclusion scenarios that involve students learning something in their own curriculum. The figure is intended to generate ongoing collaborative and strategic discussions.

Figure 11.6   Learning More About Student Populations Within an Inclusive Classroom

Students with . . .	Ideas to investigate	URLs and organizations	Other questions and ideas to investigate and next steps
Above-Average Skills	What activities are good to have on hand if students finish work ahead of their peers?	www.cectag.org www.nagc.org	
Autism Spectrum Disorders	What range of learning, social, and language abilities do students within the *spectrum* display?	www.autism-society.org www.autismspeaks.org www.asperger.org	
ADHD	Describe appropriate supports that will increase student attention.	www.chadd.org	
Cerebral Palsy	What are some physical, speech, and language considerations for students with cerebral palsy who are educated in inclusive environments?	www.ucp.org www.ncbi.nih.gov	
Communication Disorders	What are some ways educators and speech-language pathologists can coordinate lessons?	www.asha.org	
Conduct Disorders	Describe how knowing the reason for a student's behavior impacts his or her learning.	www.behavioradvisor. com/FBA.html www.nmha.org www.nimh.nih.gov	
Deafness/ Hearing Loss	What is the range of technological options available to students with hearing loss?	www.agbell.org www.shhh.org www.deafchildren.org	
Depression	What are specific signs students with depression may exhibit?	www.nimh.nih.gov	
Dyscalculia	Describe appropriate scaffolding a student with dyscalculia may need beyond the math lesson.	www.dyscalculia.org www.ldinfo.com	
Dysgraphia	Describe a type of advanced cognitive organizer that would assist students with dysgraphia.	www.ldinfo.com http://freeology.com/	

Students with . . .	Ideas to investigate	URLs and organizations	Other questions and ideas to investigate and next steps
Dyslexia	Describe ways to offer students with dyslexia more assistance to master the Common Core State Standards for English language arts.	www.interdys.org www.ortonacademy.org www.corestandards.org www.achievethecore.org	
Executive Dysfunction	What are some visual cues and cognitive strategies that would help a student with executive dysfunction?	www.schoolbehavior.com/ disorders/executive- dysfunction/	
Intellectual Disability	Identify some adaptive skills that students with intellectual disabilities achieve within inclusive classrooms.	www.thearc.org www.aaidd.org www.ndss.org	
Obsessive Compulsive Disorder (OCD)	Name some ways that students with OCD can channel unwanted behaviors into productive ones.	www.ocfoundation.org www.adaa.org	
Oppositional Defiant Disorder (ODD)	What is the value of firm, fair, and consistent rules for a student with ODD?	www.nmha.org www.mentalhealth.com	
Specific Learning Disability	Outline visual-auditory-kinesthetic-tactile (VAKT) approaches that assist students with learning disabilities within a specific subject.	www.ldanatl.org www.ncld.org	
Tourette's Syndrome	Identify some ways that educators and peers can more sensitively respond to students with Tourette's.	www.tsa-usa.org	
Traumatic Brain Injury (TBI)	Describe how to break up a lesson with a step-by-step approach for a student with a traumatic brain injury.	www.biausa.org	
Twice Exceptional	Identify what is meant by a growth versus a deficit paradigm.	http://www.hoagiesgifted. org/twice_exceptional.htm	
Visual Impairments	Identify specific auditory and tactile curriculum-related approaches for a student who has a visual impairment with either partial sight or blindness.	www.afb.org www.learningally.org/	

To review revisions in diagnostic criteria, classifications, and definitions, please consult *Diagnostic and Statistical Manual of Mental Disorders (DSM-5)* at http://www.dsm5.org/Pages/Default.aspx.

DESIGNING INCLUSION BRIDGES

We have traveled quite a distance from the time that students who displayed different intellectual, social, emotional, behavioral, physical, and communication skills received an education that isolated them from their age-level peers. Communities and educational societies have built many bridges that allow students opportunities to gain access to postsecondary achievements. This includes students achieving academic, functional, and independent living skills in heterogeneous classrooms. High expectations are no longer reserved for those students with above-average skills and levels but are now part of every child's educational objectives. Student progress on individualized education program (IEP) goals, along with current needs and levels of performance, is identified and reviewed before goals and objectives are established. Students' levels are consistently monitored to formulate plans about where and how services are delivered and the ways that progress is measured. Then collaborative groups continue the process to monitor progress and formulate plans.

Figure 11.7 Collaboration: An Essential, Continual Step

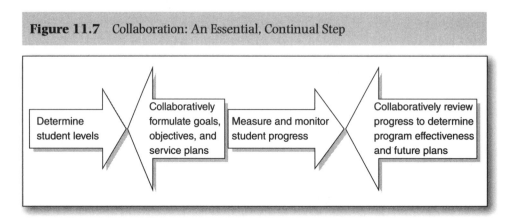

After reviewing the data, administrators, supervisors, teacher leaders, coaches, and educators figure out how to marry the research-based inclusion strategies with the curriculum. Full participation in instructional activities and assessments offers increased accountability. All parties build and maintain *inclusion bridges* to ensure ongoing staff and family communications, student participation, and collaborations between teachers, grade levels, and transitioning schools. Inclusion staff development merits knowing about students' disability characteristics and the appropriate accommodations and modifications for both instruction and assessments. As denoted by Figure 11.7, collaboration is an essential step that is continually repeated throughout the inclusive process.

12

Collaborative Interdependent Inclusion Skills

21ST CENTURY INCLUSION COMPETENCIES

Teach. Reach.
Oh, teach and reach.
Include.
Oh, yes, teach, reach, and include.

Sounds like text from a *Dick and Jane* basal reader, only those lines never would have been written years ago in a 1960s classroom. The *Dick and Jane* characters predated the federal law, the Individuals with Disabilities Education Improvement Act (IDEA) of 2004, which requires that a student with a disability be educated to the maximum extent appropriate alongside his or her peers without disabilities. The concept of inclusion and diversity was not *in vogue* back then. Today, the general education classroom with the necessary supports is looked upon as the first option of service for a student with a disability. The necessary supports include supporting the educators as well as the students. Hence, move over, Dick and Jane—it is time for classrooms to include. Welcome to the 21st century!

As we feverishly march into the 21st century, multitasking is the norm for both adults and students. The Net generation exists and thrives on technology, multimedia, social networking, and global connections. Looking beyond specific content, the curriculum standards also help students to collect, analyze, and apply information. Students need to think critically and effectively communicate and collaborate with peers. Ken Kay, president of the Partnership for 21st Century Skills, outlines that public education needs to be reconceptualized and reinvigorated (Bellanca & Brandt, 2010). This includes rethinking standards and assessments, curriculum and instruction, professional development, and learning environments. These 21st century skills compassionately and reflectively help learners with decision making, life and career skills, critical thinking skills, technology, and successes in all postsecondary performances to take the skills beyond inclusion classrooms to enter inclusive societies. Inclusion education prepares all students to critically think, communicate, care, and collaborate with effective tools.

The dilemma arises because teachers are often *co-learners* trying to keep pace with the newest technologies and the constant stream of information. It is no longer exclusively about the core subjects taught but is more about getting students to better process, remember, and apply information. Students with and without special needs often exhibit difficulties when too much information is offered too fast. The goal is to integrate higher-order thinking skills, along with effective communication and collaboration, to improve student learning beyond the school years. Educators employ newer technologies to gain students' attention to process and retain information. Podcasts, digital teaching platforms, interactive whiteboards, YouTube, Animoto, classroom Facebook pages such as Edmodo (http://www.edmodo.com/), and more engage and involve students in ways unimaginable less than five years ago. Students with autism who are nonverbal were thought to be uncommunicative, but they are now able to express their thoughts, emotions, needs, and responses through iPad apps. Students with the highest, lowest, and average abilities within heterogeneous inclusive classrooms are now educated with innovative tools. For example, AutoSummarize, available on Word tools (Microsoft, 2013) allows students to highlight and summarize the major points of information contained in a website, scientific information, a historical document, essays, or reports, while Wordle (Feinberg, 2011) offers a visual of important words and ideas in text provided.

Educators have the ability to empower students with the confidence to make effective choices as they march into the 21st century. The content standards embrace 21st century themes and skills. Themes include global awareness and financial, economic, business, entrepreneurial, civic, and health literacy. Information, media, and technology skills are no longer optional but are imperative in life and careers. Skills such as communication, collaboration, creativity, and critical thinking generate innovative students who are ongoing problem solvers. Along with these skills, students need to learn how to be flexible yet productive, take initiative, assume leadership roles, and possess both social and cross-cultural skills.

This range includes digital curricula and more universal designs within highly interactive inclusion environments. Examples include but are certainly not limited to students, educators, and families keeping daily, weekly, and monthly agendas on iPads; determining social cues by viewing an app with facial expressions; communicating via Skype or communication boards; listening to podcasts; accessing online tutorials such as Khan Academy (2012); and participating, learning, and communicating through webinars and blogs. This 21st century preparatory pedagogical approach allows students to achieve competencies for all professions and life decisions by building a critical foundation of interdisciplinary and global skills. Twenty-first century skills in turn help students to be more productive beyond the school years. Most important, the 21st century skills include functional skills, such as being punctual, honest, and dependable (Gewertz, 2007).

CREATING SHARED ENVIRONMENTS

As noted by the title of this resource, the section on 21st century skills, and many of the chapters, collaboration is essential. Professional collaboration skills include shared listening and communication. Collaborative inquiry and planning with families, educators, administrators, related staff, and all students catapult inclusion successes. Appreciative inquiry allows for open plans with individuals who volunteer contributions to invoke change (Bushe & Kassam, 2005; Kozik, Cooney, Vinciguerra, Gradel, & Black, 2009). The National Commission on Teaching and America's Future believes that team members share values and goals, collective responsibility, authentic assessments, self-directed reflection, stable settings, and strong leadership support. This includes aligning the learning needs of the student with the professional development needs of the teachers.

The Professional Development Partnership (n.d.) in New Jersey—with the collaboration of the New Jersey Association for Supervision and Curriculum Development, the New Jersey Education Association, the Center for Innovative Education at Kean University, the New Jersey Department of Education, the New Jersey Principals and Supervisors Association, the Foundation for Educational Administration, and the New Jersey Association of School Administrators—developed common language for professional learning communities. This common language is designed to communicate and plan for increased student successes, meriting tasks that allow educators to collaboratively move forward. Inclusive educators are part of this common language. The Foundation for Educational Administration connects climates of professional learning with cultures of shared leadership and the communication of high expectations for student learning. This translates to higher principal and teacher effectiveness that positively impacts the learning for students with and without exceptionalities. Leadership consortiums across our nation distribute responsibilities for everyone to work together as partners toward common goals through trusting and respectful school cultures within the structure of these types of professional communities.

Teachers are coached in ways to help both themselves and their students self-regulate learning. Maria Montessori stated, "The greatest sign of a success for a teacher . . . is to be able to say, 'The children are now working as if I did not exist'" (ThinkExist, 2012b). The same holds true for inclusion coaches and professional communities of teachers. Coaches introduce the appropriate strategies to strengthen students' levels to master the core curriculum standards, but educators are the ones who apply these interventions to their classes. In addition, in order to master any curriculum presented, students are coached to be independent thinkers. Students are therefore integral participants in inclusion coaching models within shared environments, learning to be reflective and aware learners beginning in the younger grades and onward.

Students also work cooperatively with peers to achieve new perspectives on problems while gaining improved academic and social skills (Haskell, 2000). Dialogue and interactions with peers help students to increase their cognitive thought (Fitch & Hulgin, 2008). Jean Piaget (1929) speaks about cognitive conflict and logical resolutions through cooperation by stating that children's disagreements, discussions, explanations, and persuasions with each other lead to the emergence of new positions, new ideas, and deeper thinking. Peers who talk with each other internalize cognitive processes with higher reading engagements (Fitch & Hulgin, 2009; Vygotsky 1978). Decisions collaboratively made include everyone's knowledge (Michaelsen, Bauman Knight, & Fink, 2004). The preceding statement holds true for all inclusion stakeholders.

It is also important that students with learning needs academically benefit from immediate constructive feedback (Pany & McCoy, 1988). Coaching feedback can range from immediate technological feedback (Scheeler, Congdon, & Stranbery, 2010) to reflective tête-à-têtes. Inclusion coaches continually learn and research new strategies for building relationships with teachers to help them effectively apply the best practices to their students. Nothing dramatic happens overnight, because inclusion is an evolutionary process. The inclusion seeds are planted and germinated when the educators apply the appropriate strategies and interventions to their classrooms. If the right conditions are in place, inclusion coaching is a conduit that allows the strategies to leap off the pages of the research journals to help each educator and student succeed. Diplomacy, integrity, trust, and patience are all essential ingredients that are interwoven in each and every inclusion coaching model. Most important, just as instruction needs to be differentiated, so does each inclusion coaching model. Overall, this sharing between all individuals is based on trust and respect. Shared involvements include all levels of instruction from inception to evaluation of the data as coaching roles and responsibilities for leaders, educators, and students are developed and refined.

FORMULATING PROFESSIONAL ROLES

Inclusion Teams

Professional inclusion learning communities are intended to include teams of preschool, primary, and secondary general and special education staff who work together. Like the assorted states of matter that water assumes, inclusion teams may be just as diverse in reference to their makeup and purpose. For example, preschooler educators need guidance to learn to help their students take turns or identify colors and shapes, while elementary-grade teachers plan goals to improve students' reading, writing, and math skills. Middle school and high school teachers focus on specific department proficiencies in writing within the disciplines of world history, chemistry, algebra, technical subjects, and more. Integrating essential student skills accompanies all academic, social, and functional goals and objectives. Inclusion teams include the input of related service providers, such as speech-language pathologists, occupational therapists, mobility trainers, instructional assistants, guidance counselors, school psychologists, learning consultants, social workers, behavioral intervention therapists, and support staff. Hence, a team is established to help students achieve grade-level skills, departmental objectives, core standards, and IEP-generated social, behavioral, communicative, and academic objectives. Teams need to share knowledge about disabilities by keeping current on research-based inclusion interventions to ensure that appropriate ones are applied to each and every classroom.

Inclusion teams focus on classroom and staff disability awareness activities, inclusion strategies, literature, research, peer supports, co-teaching practices, accommodations, scaffolding, resources, related staff roles, and more. Students and families are also valuable members who collaborate with schools. Peers are educated about ways to socialize with each other, capitalize on one another's strengths, and be advocates for each other. Inclusion ideas are also not restricted to one classroom or school, but professional inclusion learning communities investigate available research that includes community and global perspectives.

Teams also establish a way to assess their own progress and effectiveness as a community. According to All Things PLC (n.d.), there has to be evidence of a staff commitment to learning for all students with regard to the standards, curriculum guides, and assessments. In addition, students need to understand the criteria to monitor their learning. It does not necessarily fall into an individual teacher's lap, but collaborative teachers and teams develop mutual accountability and structured systems and cultures to help students with differing abilities and levels gain proficiencies with increased metacognition. Interdependence is then the norm for collecting, sharing, and reviewing the data, instructional choices, implementations, and student performances. Inclusion contexts direct objectives, procedures, and evaluations. Populations of students, school directives, and data influence functions and timelines.

Topics for professionals to investigate include the following:

- Classroom and staff disABILITY awareness activities
- Inclusion strategies and interventions for academics, socialization, life skills, and more
- Lesson designs for whole classes, small groups, and individuals
- Curriculum-based assessments
- Inclusion books, journals, and online research, including fiction and nonfiction genres
- Peer supports
- Co-teaching practices
- Administrative and related staff roles
- Self-advocacy activities for students
- Curriculum connections
- School-home connections
- Transitions to other units, subjects, grades, and schools
- 21st century skills
- National and global perspectives
- Legislation
- _____

A variety of team roles involve facilitators, collaborators, coaches, mentors, and researchers. If one teacher attends a workshop or learns about an effective instructional strategy, it is shared with colleagues at informal meetings, faculty workshops, grade-level meetings, and other collaborative venues. Curriculum meetings and lesson modeling are intended to enhance the skills of educators who in turn figure out ways to continually plan for and achieve student improvements. Bob Chase, a former National Education Association president, poignantly states, "Professional development is not the hood ornament; it is the engine of school improvement" (Bernhardt, 2002, p. 141).

The collaborative planners in Figure 12.1 invite staff to continually document inclusion interventions.

Inclusion Book Clubs

The next few resources delineate a sample of some professional book club choices from fiction to nonfiction genres, including magazines and journals that professionals investigate to learn more about differences. The intention is to capitalize on the knowledge from the literature to advance professional growth and, in turn, students' skills.

The listings provided in Figure 12.2 offer choices for adult reads across various genres. *RALPH* magazine (Milam, n.d.) offers an article that originally appeared in *New Mobility Magazine* with additional disability reads.

Journal and Magazine* Choices

- *Teaching Exceptional Children:* http://journals.cec.sped.org/tec

- *Disability Studies Quarterly:* http://dsq-sds.org

- *Journal of Learning Disabilities:* http://m.ldx.sagepub.com

- *Journal of Speech, Language, and Hearing Research:* http://jslhr.asha.org

- *American Journal on Intellectual and Developmental Disabilities:* http://www.aaiddjournals.org

- *Ability Magazine:* http://www.abilitymagazine.com

- *EP: Exceptional Parent:* http://www.eparent.com

- *EL: Educational Leadership:* http://www.ascd.org/publications/educational-leadership.aspx

---

* Some choices may require belonging to professional organizations with district or individual memberships.

Peer Awareness, Bibliotherapy, and Support Systems

Awareness

Increased peer awareness to generate acceptance is essential. It is imperative that students within inclusive classrooms be more knowledgeable and sensitive to their classmates and peers who have disabilities. Coaches help educators set up classrooms that promote the belief that differentiation is the norm, with all students receiving different supports, scaffolding, and enrichment opportunities based on their individual learning profiles. This means viewing students with learning, developmental, emotional, social, behavioral, and physical differences as individuals who possess many strengths.

Figure 12.1a Team Planner

Team Planner *Please attach all relevant anecdotal records, observations, additional comments, and work samples to this planner.*	Initial Planning Date: _____	Midterm Meeting Date: _____	Final Evaluations Team Date: _____
School			
Contributors			
Class/Subject(s)			
Student Information Name/Grade/Age			
Current Levels Formal and Informal Assessments			
Student Strengths			
Student Weaknesses			
Goals and Objectives Academic/Functional Social/Behavioral Emotional-Perceptual Communicative Study Skills			
Instructional Strategies			
Instructional Materials			
Frequency of Intervention			
Results			
Comments			

Figure 12.1b   Formative and Summative Progress Monitoring and Assessment Notes

Student: _____

First Quarter	Second Quarter	Third Quarter	Fourth Quarter

Figure 12.2 Books to Gain Increased Sensitivities and Knowledge About disABILITIES

Title	Author	Synopsis
House Rules	Jodi Picoult	A teenage boy with Asperger's syndrome tries to figure out crime scenes and ends up becoming the one on trial
The Dive From Clausen's Pier	Ann Packer	A relationship between two young adults changes after the boyfriend has an accident that results in his physical disability
Running With Scissors	Augusten Burroughs	The story of a boy's life growing up in an dysfunctional environment
The Memory Keeper's Daughter	Kim Edwards	A man gives away his newborn daughter who has Down syndrome
The Curious Incident of the Dog in the Night-Time	Mark Haddon	A young boy with autism investigates the death of a neighbor's dog
Still Me	Christopher Reeve	Candid memoirs from Christopher Reeve, who talks about his life before and after his paralysis
It's So Much Work to Be Your Friend: Helping the Child With Learning Disabilities Find Social Success	Richard Lavoie	Talks about the social challenges students with learning differences face and the strategies that help students learn how to succeed
Being the Other One: Growing Up With a Brother or Sister Who Has Special Needs	Kate Strohm	Speaks about the emotional challenges of siblings who have brothers or sisters with disabilities
You Will Dream New Dreams: Inspiring Personal Stories by Parents of Children With Disabilities	Stanley Klein and Kim Schive	Inspirational stories and narratives from the parents of students with disabilities who share their perspectives to inspire and inform other parents and professionals
Learning Outside the Lines: Two Ivy League Students With Learning Disabilities and ADHD Give You the Tools for Academic Success and Educational Revolution	Jonathan Mooney and David Cole	Two students who were considered *academic failures* end up collaborating as authors to talk about their perseverance to succeed despite initial learning challenges. They offer strategies for other students to succeed in college and beyond
Born on a Blue Day: Inside the Extraordinary Mind of an Autistic Savant	Daniel Tammet	A young man candidly talks about his strengths and weaknesses, including his synesthesia, a neurological syndrome that allows a person to experience numbers and words as shapes, colors, textures, and motions
The Way I See It!	Temple Grandin	An animal activist and self-advocate for autism shares her inspirational achievements
My Thirteenth Winter: A Memoir	Samantha Abeel	A girl with dyscalculia talks about the challenges she encountered in school
Embracing disABILITIES in the Classroom: Strategies to Maximize Students' Assets	Toby Karten	Ways to integrate lessons with sensitivities and strategies that maximize students' abilities by teaching through a strength paradigm. Activities for disABILITY awareness, rubrics, literature, and curriculum lessons are offered

(Continued)

Figure 12.2 (Continued)

Title	Author	Synopsis
Of Mice and Men	John Steinbeck	A friendship between two men unfolds in 1930s California
The Catcher in the Rye	J. D. Salinger	A story of the emotional turmoil experienced by a teenage boy who experiences feelings of rebellion and alienation
The Heart Is a Lonely Hunter	Carson McCullers	The novel unfolds in the deep South and discusses each character's individual personalities, inherited traits, and circumstantial experiences
Flowers for Algernon	Daniel Keyes	A man with developmental differences undergoes a radical experiment that temporarily heightens his intelligence level
Dibs in Search of Self	Virginia Axline	Play therapy sessions of a twice-exceptional young boy documented by a psychologist

Coaches help educators arrange disABILITY awareness assemblies for classes, grade levels, and school districts. People with cerebral palsy, blindness, learning differences, hearing impairments, and other differences speak with students in forums such as individual classes and grade-level assemblies. Programs such as *Kids on the Block* (2012) and visits from former students, disability awareness advocates, parents, and community members are well received by students and staff.

Gaining increased awareness helps students to embrace and better understand peers who need extra help or require alternative accommodations, modifications, and sometimes just a little more TLC. This awareness replaces criticism and bullying caused by the lack of understanding and limited exposure to the facts about how real people live their lives.

Bibliotherapy

As an option, enlist the use of fiction and nonfiction books to help students understand more about disabilities. *Embracing disABILITIES in the Classroom: Strategies to Maximize Students' Assets* (Karten, 2008a) offers novel-ties with literature choices for teachers to offer students pluralistic themes with characters who just happen to have disabilities. The instruction focuses on comprehension skills, yet the students are reading about children with disabilities who are involved in everyday situations, just like themselves. The following novel-ties offer examples of three books at different grade levels that respectively explore learning, intellectual, and hearing differences. These can be shared with teachers as models. Encourage staff to use activities and readings such as these to promote more acceptance of differences.

The Don't-Give-Up Kid and Learning Disabilities
by Jeanne Gehret

1. Why does Alex's mom call him the "don't-give-up kid"?

2. Why do you think Alex read the word *top* as *pot*?

3. Explain why Alex didn't have many friends at school.

4. Describe the difference between Mrs. Potter and Mrs. Baxter.

5. Research the inventor, Thomas Edison, telling about his school experiences.

6. How do kids get learning differences?

7. Did you ever have trouble reading?

8. What's your favorite subject in school?

9. Which school subject do you think is the toughest?

10. Describe a time you wanted to give up on something, but then figured out a way to do it.

Source: Karten, T. (2008a). *Embracing disABILITIES in the classroom: Strategies to maximize students' assets.* Thousand Oaks, CA: Corwin.

The Man Who Loved Clowns
by June Rae Wood

1. Do you know someone who is similar to Delrita's Uncle Punky?

2. If you were Delrita, do you think that you would be ashamed of Punky or have *ambivalent* feelings?

3. One of this book's themes is about dealing with grief. Describe how the characters handled some of their unfortunate situations.

4. Delrita's hobby was whittling wooden figures. Describe a product that you or a friend created.

5. Defend or argue the viewpoint that Punky was ready to live an independent life.

6. How can we as a society help everyone to realize and maximize his or her potentials?

7. Research this site (http://www.ndss.org/) and list five facts you learned about Down syndrome.

8. Describe some ways that Down syndrome can become an "up syndrome."

Source: Karten, T. (2008a). *Embracing disABILITIES in the classroom: Strategies to maximize students' assets.* Thousand Oaks, CA: Corwin.

Singing Hands
by Delia Ray (hearing differences)

1. Identify how this book's characters and plot would be different if the time setting was the present, instead of 1948.

2. Gussie's dad used a Smith Corona typewriter. Create a timeline, beginning with this typewriter, of the major innovations and discoveries that led to today's computers.

3. Gussie remarked, "The whole Negro family had to file to the colored section in the very back of the bus." Research and detail other injustices that existed due to discriminatory segregation policies in the South.

4. Identify synonyms and antonyms for each of these nouns Mrs. Fernely assigned on Gussie's first *Weekly Word List*. You can use this online source: http://www.synonym.com.

Word	Synonym	Antonym
knavery		
imprudence		
impropriety		
mortification		
perfidy		
ignominy		
acrimony		

5. Choose one of the following works of literature, operas, and poems mentioned in *Singing Hands* and write a brief synopsis that includes details about the characters, settings, and plots.
   a. *Madame Butterfly* (John Luther Long's short story or Puccini's opera)
   b. *Casey at the Bat* by Ernest Thayer
   c. *The Hunchback of Notre-Dame* by Victor Hugo
   d. *The Tell-Tale Heart* by Edgar Allan Poe
   e. *Pegasus* (the Greek myth)

6. The author, Delia Ray, notes that 1930s–1970s society ignored and often shunned the *handicapped*. Many people believed it was shameful to sign since you should disguise your disability. Respond to this viewpoint from two perspectives:
   a. A person from the *Ears*   b. Someone who is deaf

7. Delia's parents had some innovative and adaptive tools in their home such as a light bulb that was connected to a doorbell and a flashing light instead of a beep on an alarm clock that alerted them to the sounds. Investigate and identify three technological advances that have improved opportunities for people with hearing impairments and other disabilities.

8. Working with a peer, figure out what is being said when each of you sign a sentence with the alphabetic finger spelling shown in the beginning of *Singing Hands*. As a challenge, try singing and signing "The Star-Spangled Banner" with emotions, not sounds!

Source: Karten, T. (2008a). *Embracing disABILITIES in the classroom: Strategies to maximize students' assets*. Thousand Oaks, CA: Corwin.

These online sites offer book choices to investigate to help both educators and students learn more about ADHD, autism, blindness, cerebral palsy, deafness, Down syndrome, and learning, intellectual, and physical differences.

Polk Library: http://www.uwosh.edu/library/emc/Bibliographies/disabilities.pdf

Teacher Vision: http://www.teachervision.fen.com/learning-disabilities/reading/5316.html

Support Systems

Just as teachers form collaborative teams, when peers act as teams, the collaboration yields higher results. Peers without disabilities offer peers with disabilities academic and social-related supports (Bond & Castagnera, 2006; Carter, Moss, Hoffman, Chun, & Sisco, 2011; Jimenez, Browder, Spooner, & DiBiase, 2012; Mastropieri, Scruggs, & Berkeley, 2007). Types of peer support for students with mild to more severe disabilities include the following:

- One-on-one tutoring
- Peer assistance
- Cooperative learning
- Classwide peer tutoring

Peer assistance occurs in many settings, ranging from classes that teach reading, mathematics, biology, physical education, or ceramics, to assemblies, the cafeteria at lunch, recess, and traveling on a school bus. It includes peers offering help with directions, reading more difficult text or vocabulary, encouraging social interactions, and more. The type of assistance depends on the nature of a disability. Some students need help getting started, some need help keeping pace, and other students need extra review or encouragement.

The Center for Effective Collaboration and Practice (n.d.) offers substantive research on the benefits of systems such as classwide peer tutoring along with ideas on how teachers can capitalize on the strengths of their students. Peers clarify questions, encourage students to finish assignments, and offer opportunities for students of all ability levels to experience increased practice and learning.

Peers who support each other capitalize and honor one another's individualities and strengths. This is evidenced as students work together in cooperative groups as peer mentors, coaches, and learning collaborators. Peer training includes staff sharing rationales, expectations, activities and strategies for learning, feedback, and communications to promote increased successful interactions and access to the general education curriculum (Carter & Kennedy, 2006). When peers are compassionate, aware, and reflective of their actions toward one another, there is no inclusion pecking order.

The next section offers educator, curriculum, and classroom examples and realities.

PART V

Inclusion Coaching Realities

13

Response to Inclusion Interventions

Identifying essential knowledge and skills that students need to know requires professional and collaborative observing, monitoring, planning, and evaluating with shared responsibilities and ownership of decisions and tasks. For example, a standard is identified and described in terms of rigor, prerequisite skills, how and when it is taught, ways mastery will be determined, and opportunities for extension (Buffum, Mattos, & Weber, 2012). Many students within inclusive classrooms require interventions that allow the learning standards to be revisited at set times during the year to ensure retention and generalization. If a sixth-grade student demonstrated his or her ability to provide a concluding written statement or section that follows from an argument in October, that does not mean that the student will not need a review of this standard in February to ensure retention. Teaching and reinforcing good study skills and appropriate peer interactions involve more than a 15-minute mention during the first week of school if these skills are expected to be refined. Math skills spiral, but reinforcement of basic facts with opportunities for practice, application, and generalization is essential. Planning for these opportunities means that everyone from principals to educators, teaching assistants, students, and families values the learning process to ensure that the interventions are appropriately leveled, scheduled, and reinforced.

LIFELONG PROGRESS

In addition, students need interventions that help them develop self-regulatory behaviors that create lifelong behavioral, social, and emotional skills, whether a student plans to attend a college or begin a job following high school. These include, but are not limited to, goal setting, organization, motivation, demonstrating rule-governed behavior that limits impulsivity, and exhibiting social reciprocity. Both academic and social behaviors need to be identified, monitored, and responded to with the appropriate coaching interventions. Progress monitoring then yields appropriate interventions that include minimizing or extending support. Inclusion is an ongoing collaborative process that goes beyond monitoring students, but helps students and educators develop interventions to continually become self-regulated learners who strategize to realistically acknowledge, plan, and monitor progress. Encouraging this behavior requires inclusion protocols that value reinforcement schedules, praise, differentiation, flexibility, and structure.

Academics and behavior often hold hands, since some students act out, rather than admit that they do not understand something. Coaches assist educators in identifying the causes of behavior with functional behavioral assessments (FBA). This takes into account where and when behavior occurs and all variables involved. Behavioral intervention plans (BIP) are often put into place to determine appropriate antecedents and replace negative behavior whether a student is seeking more control, attention from teachers or peers, or escape from tasks that are too difficult or too easy. Creating schoolwide, classroom, and individual behavioral expectations, such as being respectful and responsible whether one is walking in a hallway, eating lunch, or writing a summary of *Tomás and the Library Lady* (Mora, 1997) or *To Kill a Mockingbird*, is essential. In addition, supports for encouraging positive behaviors range from structured token economy systems for students with more intellectual needs to individual student monitoring, conferencing, and classwide or school celebrations. Student-friendly environments have rules posted with concise purposes and directions to ensure on-task behavior. Again, interventions will vary, depending on student levels and needs from written to verbal cues or prompts to private signals, family and peer supports, additional modeling, and scaffolding. School leaders investigate and infuse character education programs such as Project Wisdom (2013) and Character Counts (Josephson Institute, 2012) to value and promote ethical and respectful traits in their students.

Inclusive partners problem-solve to determine students' academic, emotional, social, behavioral, and communicative levels to determine appropriate interventions and inclusive decisions. These interventions are not arbitrarily chosen but are based on specific student-generated needs and levels. If students do not respond to these interventions in the general education classroom, then more interventions inside or outside the inclusive classroom are investigated and given within a higher tier of intensive research-based supports. Stagnation is never an option since response to intervention (RTI) is an ongoing, fluid process. The RTI planning form in Part I (see Figure 2.4) outlines a structured way for teams to consistently monitor student progress within an inclusive classroom.

14

Relating to Educators

There is a vast difference between inclusion coaching and inclusion hand-holding. Ultimately, teachers and students are the ones who need to take the *learning shots*. An inclusion coach promotes independence and wants the interventions to belong to the educators and students. Inclusion coaches guide teachers, model strategies, and offer collaborative support. Inclusion coaches and school leaders often answer questions with reflective questions that encourage educators to think about their own solutions with constructivist discoveries and classroom applications. Trusting relationships between educators and administrators and coaches are built over time. One morning while conversing with an administrator, a perfect nonexample of inclusion support was discovered. Inclusion coaching is not the *FBI*—in this case *the Federal Bureau of Inclusion!* It is not about the act of catching teachers being noncompliant, but it is about assisting educators in their arduous efforts to deliver the curriculum to diverse learners. In addition, using a cookie-cutter approach will not work either, since each situation is a unique one. Inclusion Band-Aids do not miraculously heal each student's or educator's inclusion needs, but collaborative decisions are individually prescribed. Figure 14.1 relates coaching to each teacher's curriculum.

Figure 14.1 Inclusion Curriculum Coaching Connections

Algebra	There are many variables involved in each inclusion equation.
O. Henry	Surprise endings are to be circumvented at all costs.
Photosynthesis	The right ingredients are imperative to ensure that positive energy is produced.

(Continued)

Figure 14.1 (Continued)

Bill of Rights	Inclusion is an ongoing process, with necessary amendments provided.
Dance	Collaborative partners choreograph their dance steps without stepping on one another's toes.
Chorus	Just as a chorus comprises a range of voices, such as soprano, alto, baritone, and bass, diverse inclusive contributing voices are honored.

INCLUSION COACHING VIGNETTES, LETTERS, AND CURRICULUM EXAMPLES

The following introductory letter communicates a message to a staff and can be used as a model if an outside coach or consultant is introduced to the teachers.

Dear Inclusion Setting Teachers,

We are very happy to announce that arrangements have been made to provide you with an opportunity to address collaboration, planning, strategies, and interventions in the inclusive classroom. _____, an expert in the field, will be our consultant to work with you as we continue to improve our inclusion setting classrooms across the district.

We are currently in the process of setting up brief a.m. meetings in respective buildings to offer you a chance to meet her/him before she/he visits your classroom and/or a collaborative session is scheduled. At that time and continuing in your collaborative sessions, _____ will share in more detail her/his role in working with you in a nonevaluative coaching format. She/He will provide you with resources that you and your grade-level teams will be able to continually access for more information about inclusion, specific disabilities, and effective co-teaching practices. Your candid communications, along with the survey you complete, will help guide her/his work with you to help strengthen your inclusive classrooms and co-teaching partnerships.

Basically, after the kickoff meetings, _____ will be in all the schools during the week of _____. She/He will be observing a few classrooms informally and then holding collaborative team planning/inclusion coaching sessions. She/He will then return on _____ to revisit and answer your questions during additional collaborative inclusion co-teaching sessions. The inclusion professional development will conclude with a closure meeting on _____ at ____.

This is an exciting opportunity, and I know that you will embrace _____ expertise and find the experience rewarding!

The following vignette offers a brief snapshot of one day in the life of an inclusion coach.

An Inclusion Coaching Day

I walked into Ms. M. Brace's room early in the morning before her 11th-grade first-period students arrived. We had scheduled time for our collaborative planning session to share lesson feedback. She greeted me with a smile and remarked that she loved applying the writing concepts shared during last week's inclusion kickoff workshop. We spoke about formulating a behavioral plan for one of the students and how to record the data. Plans were made to revisit the teacher at another collaborative planning session scheduled the following week.

Next period, I visited a middle school social studies class that, in addition to the general education teacher, had a co-teacher and an assistant in the room circulating and exchanging ideas with the students in whole class and small group scenarios. The students were learning about the Shang Dynasty and involved in cooperative projects. As an outsider observing, I had a difficult time identifying which teacher was the general educator or special educator and which students were classified. Roles were interchanged, and no one was singled out. All students were smiling and attentive. I circulated about as well, answering student questions and offering praise.

I then touched base with a math teacher, Mr. A. Pathy, who informed me that he did not need any coaching help at all with his inclusion class. I was welcome to stay, but it did not matter since he was retiring this year. He then showed a video to the class. Some students watched, some took notes, and some slept. We scheduled a debriefing time.

Later in the day I met with several middle school teachers who shared a common planning period. We addressed prior communicated concerns about ways to include a student they shared who was diagnosed with autism. The instructional assistant also attended. Together, we decided on specific academic and social goals to capitalize on this student's musical and technology strengths. We formulated ideas on ways to increase appropriate peer interactions and class participation with cooperative assignments. As a professional community of learners, we decided that the student would design and share with his peers WebQuests and flashcards he created online to increase his attention, motivation, and social skills. The English, history, math, and science teachers also agreed to assign a cross-disciplinary unit on the Industrial Revolution. Structured guidelines would be outlined in a rubric to divide the long-range project into intermittent checks to ensure mastery and completion of all tasks. The teachers communicated with the instructional assistant on ways that she could help the student to gain skills, without creating power struggles or overdependence. Time helping the music teacher would be offered as a reward for completed assignments. The teachers' years of experience ranged from a first-year teacher to those who had been teaching for more than 25 years. The 55-minute collaborating planning period was a productive one.

During the last period, I met with a team of third-grade teachers who were not receptive to inclusion coaching within a professional learning community (PLC) since their prior experiences were unproductive ones. In the past, they were required to fill out forms and establish PLC agreed-upon norms and meeting times, but there was no classroom application or follow-through. Often some of the special educators were arbitrarily assigned to another PLC if the special education teacher taught more than one grade. Some years the teachers communicated that they wrote professional plans that the administration signed off on that never mentioned the students at all. I explained that our professional inclusion

(Continued)

(Continued)

meetings would be specifically designed to improve inclusion knowledge with appropriate classroom strategies and interventions for the students. We brainstormed ideas and agreed to prioritize student study skills, fluency, and establishing better home support as the three areas that we would focus on during the upcoming marking periods. Additional meetings were scheduled, and baseline levels would be recorded with rating scales, administered developmental reading assessments, and communication logs. Once structure was established, attitudes toward the inclusion coaching concept improved immensely.

When inclusion relationships are established, the coaching often takes a serendipitous course. As an example, I shared a resource that offered strategies for students with learning disabilities with one teacher who then decided that the rest of the seventh-grade teachers would benefit greatly from the intervention list. He then provided each teacher with his or her own copy to reference. Another time, a learning disabilities teacher consultant wanted to collaborate with the classroom teachers and inclusion coach to monitor and record the reading levels of students who went from resource center settings to inclusive co-taught ones to note what impact the inclusion setting had on the students' reading levels. Inclusion coaching shares the responsibilities and knowledge. It also allows teachers to internalize and apply the strategies to their unique population of students and, most important, coach each other in the process.

In addition, technology offers excellent ways to coach, communicate, and share ideas. The following e-mails present digital inclusion coaching communications, the first of which was sent to teachers in response to their shared surveys.

Thanks for forwarding these surveys; they will be extremely helpful in our coaching sessions. The candid responses you offer will be explored and validated in our professional development activities and your professional learning communities. We will be emphasizing collaborative inclusion practices that connect to your students with differentiated lessons.

This next e-mail transcript was feedback communicated to an administrator after teachers in several schools and classrooms in the district participated in inclusion coaching.

What a whirlwind of a week! Although each situation is unique, the classrooms that I visited and the majority of the teachers that I collaborated and planned with were receptive to the inclusion ideas and resources offered. Now, I truly hope that the application is evidenced across the curriculum and schools.

We explored how good teaching practices via the inclusion strategies are applicable for all levels of students, without sacrificing one group's needs for another.

Co-teaching models and curriculum ideas were shared. Revisitations with many of the teachers to continue the inclusion thrust and to see how some of the suggestions have been concretely applied are scheduled.

The professional development session next month will solidify all and continue to plant inclusion seeds to help both the general and special education teachers collaborate, plan, and apply the inclusion principles with their respective teams of teachers. If our first meeting was the kickoff, I hope that we will then be able to celebrate a few touchdowns at the next sessions!

The next e-mail was in response to a special educator who wanted more ways to increase his effectiveness as a co-teacher. During my observations his body language and minimal involvement had reflected how uncomfortable he was with his inclusion role.

OK, here are some co-teaching suggestions for your classes:

- When the general education teacher is leading, as we discussed, physical circulation is essential.
- Your sheer proximity increases student focus, attention, and motivation. Of course, when you circulate and assist, you are as inconspicuous as possible, helping all of the students without singling out any individual students. The extent will depend upon the lesson topics and classroom arrangements. Gentle reminders and *the look* work wonders, too!
- You can also scribe teacher directions and/or highlight major lesson points on the whiteboard at the class onset (e.g., lesson objectives). During the lesson emphasize the key points and/or directions (e.g., open to page XX). As a brief 5-minute closure either verbally or in writing always ensure students' understandings (e.g., "Let's review what we learned today") and ask leading questions (e.g., "What if …?") and distribute exit cards.
- Having the lesson plans ahead of time allows us to prepare appropriate graphic organizers, writing frames, outlines of math steps/formulas, specific problem examples with step-by-step rules outlined, and multisensory-VAKT (visual-auditory-kinesthetic-tactile) applications for the English and math lessons. Post preview or review notes on your website.
- Offer appropriate scaffolding to the students (e.g., transitional or sensory word lists, monthly calendars that outline due dates, models of math problems, formula sheets, interim checks of student work for long-range assignments, monitor note taking). Always keep in mind that fine line between helping and enabling.
- Discuss with your co-teachers if they want you to teach a parallel, review, or study skill lesson once a week, if the depth of the topic requires additional practice. This can be with small groups or the whole class.
- Continue to offer to share responsibilities (e.g., parent contact, grading assessments).
- Always try to generate critical thinking skills by joining the teachers in their Socratic classroom discussions by bouncing ideas off each other to generate more student involvement.
- As we discussed, each class and student presents unique needs and specific strategies. Yet, if you visit my website at www.inclusionworkshops.com and click on the Principles tab, those 18 inclusive principles are the ones that we as educators always try to creatively apply.
- Ms. N, Mrs. P, and Mrs. D are fortunate to have you there to ensure that the lessons are reaching *all* of the students. These co-teaching reminders are no longer my strategies, but now yours! :-) See you next week to talk more, but definitely share any thoughts or concerns before then, too!

This brief e-mail was sent to another co-teacher who was on the right track, but just needed a bit more confidence and affirmation.

> Hi O,
>
> Thank you for taking the time to collaborate together last week and welcoming me into your classrooms, in between your pack-filled schedule! I hope that the co-teaching and inclusion ideas that we reviewed will be helpful to you and your co-teacher and the students in your class. As we discussed, each situation varies, but we both certainly agree that the students greatly benefit from your vigilant eyes to continually show their best.
> Good luck with all!

The next e-mails were generated after a collaborative meeting. An educator requested help with reformatting a test. Specific suggestions were offered, and a revised document was sent.

> Thank you for your kind words of encouragement and recognizing how inclusion does work for many of us. I did talk to you about reviewing some of the tests that I have made to go along with our literature units. I have attached two. One is for our fifth-grade fantasy unit—we focus on the story elements with this novel. The other is sixth-grade adversity where we focus on several literary elements along with the story elements. Any feedback would be appreciated.
>
> Hi M,
>
> I am glad that we had a chance to have an *inclusion chat!* The attached documents offer a few suggestions for the tests you sent. I basically reworded a few questions, placed fewer questions on a page, switched the matching to eliminate more reading requirements, and offered a few different types of questions that integrated other skills (e.g., drawing a picture, creating a poem, writing a newspaper article). It's yours to play with and tweak with your co-teachers since you know your students best. In the interim, enjoy the rest of the week, and I look forward to our continued collaboration!

The next few curriculum examples offer general and special educators ways to tweak their assignments. These models do not change the student outcomes or dilute the requirements, but they offer students the information in smaller bites with more visuals and less jargon.

A first-year teacher offered the following creative social studies assignment to her sixth-grade class, but the format was not *student-friendly*. Together we created graphic organizers that compartmentalized the requirements and offered the students language frames to organize their writing and fulfill all parameters of the assignment. See Figure 14.2.

Figure 14.2   Sixth-Grade Social Studies Assignment: Original and
Compartmentalized

Egyptian Artifact Project

Date Given:_____

Due Dates: _____ (Description) and (Final Project)

   Congratulations! You and your team of archaeologists have just made an incredibly amazing find! You have uncovered an artifact from Ancient Egypt. The class cannot wait to see what you have found!

   Your job for this project is to first decide on the category and type of the item you have found. The item can range from a pair of golden sandals that have been worn by a specific pharaoh, to a religious article or perhaps an egg carton re-creation of the Egyptian game of senet (the ancestor of backgammon), to a replica of the gold mask of King Tutankhamen, to another choice. Once you decide what item you are going to re-create, write a description of it. (Hint: There are many topics to include, so you will probably need to include more than one paragraph.)

You must include:

* A description of the item.
* Who in Ancient Egypt would have used the item.
* What time period the item is from.
* The purpose of the item. (What was it used for?)
* What materials the Ancient Egyptians used to make the item. (For example, the Egyptians needed gold to make the sandals, but how did they shape it?)
* Where exactly you found it—be creative. (Was it in a tomb, or did you find it buried by the river? Did you find it in Upper or Lower Egypt?) Including a map is optional.
* How you re-created the item.
* The description is due _____.

   Your final product, the artifact, is your re-creation of a real item. For example, you do not need to figure out how to shape gold to make the sandals or jewelry. You would find an alternative way to make them. The artifact is due on _____. You should be ready to share your archaeological find on this exciting day in front of your classmates/fellow archaeologists!

   The following are some websites to help you. (Type in "Egypt" in the search bar, and you will find many entries in the sites below.)

* www.pbs.org
* www.nationalgeographic.com
* www.metmuseum.org/
* http://ngm.nationalgeographic.com/2005/06/king-tut/mysteries/resources

---

Source: Adapted from sixth-grade social studies teacher Nancy Billyer.

Requirements compartmentalized:

Project Requirements: Create an Egyptian artifact	Notes/Answer
1. **Describe** the object.	
2. Describe **who** in Ancient Egypt would use the item.	

(Continued)

(Continued)

Project Requirements: Create an Egyptian artifact	Notes/Answer
3. Name the time period.	
4. Tell its **purpose (use)**.	
5. Identify **materials** needed to make the artifact.	
6. Identify the **location** where the item was **found**.	
7. Describe **how you created (made)** the artifact.	

The next language frame was offered to the students to organize their thoughts. After the students filled in the lines, they were encouraged to add more sentences and then required to rewrite the entire piece either by hand or as a Word document.

Social Studies Artifact Project

For my artifact project, I decided to create a _____. This was used by ancient Egyptians to _____. If I was to describe this object, I would say that it _____. The object is found during the time period _____.

Ancient Egyptians used the object in the following ways.

This object was found by _____.

The Egyptians used many materials to create this item, such as the following:

_____

_____

_____

_____

There were several steps to create this item. First, _____. Next, _____.

Afterwards, _____. Finally, _____.

I re-created this object by _____.

I learned more about _____ and _____ when I created this object.

This next chart was offered to a high school physics teacher to assist students with compartmentalizing basic concepts for notes.

Symbol	What does the letter represent?	How is it measured?
F	Force (push or pull on an object)	Newtons
m	Mass (measure of amount of material or atoms in an object)	kg (kilograms)
a	Acceleration (rate at which an object changes its position)	2 m/s
F = ma translates to Force = Mass × Acceleration Forces in my life include _____.		

This outline was shared with an English teacher who wanted to offer his students more organization to preplan essays.

Thesis Statement I look forward to getting a job <div align="right">Page 1</div>	**Reason 1** More money for myself and family <div align="right">Page 2</div>
Reason 2 Experience <div align="right">Page 3</div>	**Reason 3** Independence <div align="right">Page 4</div>

The next educator asked for feedback on a journalism assignment.

Hi R,

Wow, what an incredible amount of work you put into this creative project! I admire that the assignment is so highly structured with all elements and expectations clearly outlined; however, I could understand why several of the students were overwhelmed. Some vocabulary requires further explanation. For example, you state: "The lead uses a method appropriate to the story." Students' definition of the word *appropriate* varies. Another statement, "Comic must be existential," is too vague. I loved the visuals and models you offered, but I wonder if it would be best to first offer each of the required elements in smaller bites, with students practicing one aspect of the assignment at a time, before the whole project was presented to them. Perhaps that could be accomplished in structured *journalism centers*. After students were proficient with each one, receiving a packet such as this would then contain material within their prior knowledge. As I mentioned, always break up assignments into their parts and monitor steps toward completion at interim dates, before the entire project is due.

Again, your organization is incredible, including the fact that both co-teachers' names are on the packet! Your high expectations are also terrific, but as teachers we sometimes need to determine that fine line between challenging students to perform their best and offering the appropriate scaffolding that allows that to happen.

Also, please remember that even though some students had difficulties with the assignment, a tremendous amount of learning occurred. You planted many writing seeds! I hope that this feedback helped; keep the line of communication open.

The next few e-mails were sent to communities of learners who wanted answers to specific questions after one- or two-day workshops at varying inner-city, rural, and suburban school districts. I always offer my e-mail address as a way to say that inclusion is more than a snapshot process.

First is an e-mail to a Spanish teacher who requested more resources.

Hi ST,

I am glad that we had time for the planning session during the workshop. Those strategies that your staff collaboratively investigated are applicable across the disciplines, including Spanish! As promised, here are a few additional content-specific sites for you to review:

Spanish for Kids: http://www.123teachme.com/learn_spanish/spanish_for_children

Highlights: http://www.highlightskids.com/Stories/Rebus/rebus_desertDoves/0606_desertDoves.asp

Cultural Bridges: http://writing.colostate.edu/guides/teaching/esl/cultural.cfm

Principles for Culturally Responsive Teaching: http://www.alliance.brown.edu/tdl/tl-strategies/crt-principles.shtml

Interesting Things for ESL Students: http://www.manythings.org/

Teaching Tolerance: http://www.tolerance.org/activities

These are the cards I spoke about:

Spanish in a Flash from Edupress: http://www.highsmith.com/edupress/Spanish-in-a-Flash-Flash-Cards-Set-2-EP2343-c_21710710/EP2343/

Additional resources:

http://www.bookslibros.com/SpanishForNinos.htm

http://dictionary.reverso.net/english-spanish/rebus

http://translate.google.com/m/translate

http://www.brainpopesl.com/

http://quizlet.com/subject/spanish/

Good luck with all!

Next is communication to a support teacher who had curriculum concerns.

Hi CC,

I am responding to your inquiry regarding how to teach grade-level standards when students have not mastered the curriculum from the prior years. That is an ongoing concern of many teachers.

As we discussed later on in the workshop, it is imperative to establish a baseline level for your students to determine if gains are achieved. If they do not reach mastery, then you document their levels and revisit. I know, easier said than done. Please keep in mind that inclusion is a process and research supports that when students are placed in inclusion settings, their exposure to the grade-level standards increases both social and academic skills. Please review the Common Core State Standards website at http://www.corestandards.org/ to get a clear understanding of the grade-level expectations. Share these with your class in student-friendly language.

As we also mentioned, classroom stations, cooperative learning, multiple intelligences, thematic units, universal design for learning, and problem-based learning allow students and educators opportunities to work individually and in smaller groups to master curriculum areas that often require additional attention.

I hope that the resources I shared will also assist in your efforts. These next two sites offer ideas about disability topics and research-based inclusion practices:

http://nichcy.org/

http://ies.ed.gov/ncee/wwc/

Good luck with all; have a great summer!

Another educator wanted to know what to do if the disabilities are not visible ones.

Hi,

I am responding to your workshop inquiry about hidden disabilities. Sometimes these are the students who scream the loudest. For example, students with depression need to be acknowledged with appropriate sensitivities, attention, and creative outlets. Just because you cannot see a disability as you would if a person uses a wheelchair or for a student with Down syndrome, it does not mean that there are no signs. Signs are often apparent with changes in attitude, clothes, behavior, writings, artwork, and more. A student with a disability that you may not see, such as a child with a learning difference, dyslexia, depression, traumatic brain injury, or an executive processing disorder, needs to be frequently checked for understandings and offered accommodations, the same way that you would offer more visuals for a student with deafness, tactile opportunities for a student who is blind, step-by-step explanations and more repetition to a student with an intellectual disability, or perhaps more breaks if a student's physical stamina differs.

The following link, http://www.ist.hawaii.edu/training/hiddendisabilities/05_hidden_disabilities.php, offers additional insights.

Good luck with your inclusion efforts!

An educator and mother of a student with autism wanted more information and resources.

Hi EM,

It was a pleasure meeting you this month. As promised, here are some autism websites and resources that offer links to research, organizations, family perspectives, and educational strategies. I also copied the director, Mr. BB, of the Pennsylvania school I mentioned, who is delighted to communicate more with you about his school's inclusion practices, philosophies, and future directions. EM, meet BB!

My best to both of you!

http://www.polyxo.com/socialstories/

http://www.autism-resources.com/links/index.html

http://www.autism-society.org/

http://www.autismspeaks.org/family-services/resource-library

http://www.templegrandin.com/

http://www.cdc.gov/ncbddd/autism/index.html

Ian's Walk by Laurie Lears

My Friend With Autism by Beverly Bishop

Not My Boy! by Rodney Peete

My Brother Charlie by Holly Robinson Peete and Ryan Elizabeth Peete

My Brother Kevin Has Autism by Richard Carlson

Mockingbird by Kathryn Erskine

A speech pathologist with a caseload of students had concerns about how to have an effective role within an inclusive environment.

I am responding to your query from the workshop about your options on how to implement inclusion as a speech pathologist. You noted that you work with 78 students in four schools and do not want to overwhelm the teachers.

The crucial ingredient is to establish ongoing communication with the teachers regarding the lessons and student needs. Of course, your services are dependent on specific areas students need help with (e.g., articulation, language, fluency). Definitely encourage your teachers to send you copies of their lessons or the topics that they will be reviewing so that you can offer help to preteach the vocabulary and big ideas behind the concepts. If the students will be working in cooperative groups or need more pragmatic language skills, there needs to be a coordination between settings and a healthy range of both structure and flexibility between yourself and the general education teacher. Your range of services will vary and involve the following:

- Individual and small-group services
- Classroom consultation services (e.g., appropriate technology offered, ways to monitor progress)
- Input about ways to incorporate speech skills in class lessons
- Collaboration with planning, instruction, and assessments
- Team teaching or co-teaching within the classroom

Of course, the American Speech-Language-Hearing Association (http://www.asha.org/slp/) offers excellent ideas and resources.
Good luck with your ongoing efforts!

Another administrator was concerned with just what an inclusion PLC scenario involves. I responded to her specific queries as shown in the e-mails below.

Administrative query:

Will there be a need for substitute teachers for you to collaboratively meet with the teachers to formulate PLC plans?

When does team conferencing with you take place? I ask only because the previous director ran into some difficulty with teachers not wanting to give up prep time.

Response:

Each inclusion coaching situation varies. Collaboration can occur with the teachers during their prep time, but if this has been an issue in your district, then arranging for full- or half-day rotating substitutes or inviting the teachers to schedule their times would be the best avenues. We will directly survey teachers for the best days/hours to meet and plan, and then arrange coaching schedules around those times. Best approach is to first spend time with the educators and students in the classrooms during the lessons and then meet with teachers for the coaching sessions to determine inclusion goals and objectives. Teachers are also surveyed and encouraged to continually share specific inclusion concerns. Sometimes, meetings are arranged with grade-level teachers, with specific departments, or one-to-one. Scheduling this time is crucial for reflections and to move forward with inclusion plans. The ideal co-teaching scenario is when the special education teacher is able to conference together with the general education teachers he or she is working with. Again, once I have exact schedules of class and prep times, we can work out all details. Other situations in the past have required more than one meeting over an extended period of time to talk and tweak implementation with specific teachers and teams. Our inclusion goals are to first identify needs, then plan and assess accordingly with individual and collaborative teachers interacting as professional learning communities. The more flexible we are, the more inviting inclusion becomes!

As this small sample of staff development and inclusion coaching vignettes indicates, inclusion presents unique strengths and challenges. These communications and examples are not intended to dictate practices to teachers, but instead invite educators to ask the applicable questions that will help them be better inclusive educators. Organizing purposes and structure, while establishing trusting and positive attitudes toward inclusion and co-teaching, is the first step in coaching educators.

15

Embracing Achievements

DUPLICATING INCLUSION SUCCESSES

"Being different does not entitle you to give up or believe in excuses," said an award-winning student. Embracing the world with contagious can-do attitudes, combined with family and educational support systems, children with disabilities repeatedly said, "Yes I can!" at the 90th Conference of the Council for Exceptional Children (CEC) in Denver, Colorado, in 2012. Passionate, fearless, energetic, determined, and enthusiastic lives were revealed.

As I was walking in the convention corridor to present a session on the topic of *facilitating inclusion*, a young woman in a wheelchair approached me and asked where a room number was located. I told her that it was on the lower level and that I thought there was an elevator around the corner from the escalator we were nearing. I did not even finish my sentence before she sprinted before me, full steam ahead, and fearlessly positioned herself backwards in her wheelchair on the escalator. I followed her and walked onto the same escalator with a rolled suitcase that with trepidation I placed on the step above my feet, as I hesitantly descended. This young woman had what was perceived to be a disability, but her determination and confidence enabled her to leap forward. Speaking with individuals with exceptionalities and the people who are part of their support systems at the convention revealed how students with disabilities reach their achievements, despite what some people perceive to be flaws or imperfections. Educators, families, and students turn the unlikely into not only the possible but also the remarkable.

Yes I Can is an awards ceremony that recognizes students for their achievements in the categories of academics, arts, athletics, school and community activities, self-advocacy, technology, and transition. The 2012 CEC conference honored the lives of 29 young individuals with disabilities. I listened to students' stories and heard perspectives from parents, family members, educators, friends, and community partners, as I searched for some common threads that make up their unique tapestry. Armed with Kleenex in one hand and my iPad stylus in the other, I attentively recorded how these students spun their disabilities into accomplishments.

Laughter, tears, smiles, frustrations, and moments of uncertainty are common factors that were presented by William Bodgan, the *Yes I Can* Master of Ceremonies. Students' families and people in their support systems communicated that these young individuals devote their lives to being role models for other students with and without disabilities. Programs were handed out, and the next two hours revealed how these students evolved into successful individuals. Their everyday lives are beyond exemplary as they approach each day with gusto and a positive outlook that say "Move over world, I have arrived!"

A 20-year-old from Fort Lauderdale, Florida, diagnosed with autism, a disorder usually noted for communication impairments, is a public speaker in two languages. Another student, age 17, from Ketchikan, Alaska, who has osteopetrosis, a rare bone disorder, is her school's student council secretary and an accomplished singer. She entertained an audience of more than 100 family members and friends during the dinner reception. An 18-year-old young lady with Down syndrome is an accomplished athlete in bowling, swimming, speed skating, soccer, and track and field. A young lady, age 18, who has ataxia, a disorder that affects motor coordination, stemming from a traumatic brain injury, asserts that drawing calms her down and shakes away life's struggles. Another student, who has limited motor capabilities, sat in a wheelchair, with an initiative spirit, and was recognized for her role in school and community activities. "Just because you have a disability doesn't mean you can't try your best," she stated. A girl who is now 14 years old lost her sight at age 5, but her fearless determination allows her to embrace challenges, as she participates in the marching band, forensics team, drama club, and reading competition team. A student who has cleft lip and palate is a public speaker. "Never give up," says one of the award winners, who has multiple disabilities.

At an interview panel the next day, some of the students and their families elaborated more details. Several of the family members shared how they continually reach out to their children's teachers to help them understand their sons' and daughters' abilities.

> "Some of the people I've dealt with have PhDs, but my three letters are M-O-M and I have to trust my intuition," shared one mother.

> "My son has a great deal of compassion and resiliency," says a mom.

Her son has a rare medical condition of congenital bilateral perisylvian syndrome and is basically nonverbal, but his animated expressions at the ceremony communicated his sense of humor to the audience.

> "Take the time to learn more about disabilities, and do not put people into categories," said one dad.

> "The world needs our children," stated another dad on the panel.

Other family members, including parents and siblings, spoke about sleep deprivation, ongoing struggles, compassion, patience, and persevering attitudes. The students themselves told how they learn to understand their own strengths and interests.

"There are days that I look normal, but sometimes there is so much I do not understand. When the teacher asks for questions, I don't know what questions to ask," shared a young man with a learning disability.

"My strengths have weaknesses; capture our interests," shared a student.

"Look at me, not my disability. I was made this way for a reason, to show that having a disability doesn't make you different."

Disability lessons are offered from their stories, which can be accessed online from CEC's site (2013c). Each year, CEC honors the accomplishment of exceptional children. More information can be accessed at CEC's website (www .cec.sped.org/yesican).

Self-awareness, proactivity, goal setting, perseverance, the presence and use of support systems, and emotional coping strategies are six success attributes that were identified in a 20-year study of students with learning disabilities. LD OnLine offers the results in a guide for parents (Raskind & Goldberg, 2005). The study also denotes the lack of research that says just how to teach these skills.

"There is a balance between helping, doing for, and supporting," stated Pamela Lowry, an assistant professor from Georgian Court University, at a CEC dinner reception.

The complexity of factors with teachers, environments, students, and topics involved in the special education process can be viewed on YouTube (see "InclusionEducation channel," n.d.).

The stories of individuals with disabilities, besides those who attended this ceremony, reveal many successful lives of people who fearlessly and successfully forge ahead to accomplish great feats.

"It is sometimes the fear that holds you back," said Dan, a young man in a wheelchair who went parachuting. His story can be accessed online (see PORTCO, 2010).

Clay Marzo, who has Asperger's and is one of the world's best surfers, connects his visual skills with the water's sensations. His story can be accessed at online as well (see Marzo, 2010).

Ludwig Van Beethoven, an accomplished composer, did not hear the audience applaud his works after he became deaf. Albert Einstein, Henry Winkler, Walt Disney, and Whoopi Goldberg are just a few individuals with dyslexia who have accomplished incredible feats from the sciences to the arts. Temple Grandin, an autism advocate and accomplished animal scientist who has autism, discusses the importance of early interventions and support systems. Her life insights are given at UCtelevision (2008). *Disabled World Towards Tomorrow* offers more examples of famous people who have disabilities and can be accessed online (see Disabled World, 2006).

School systems today are advocating that students with disabilities be included in general education classes and exposed to the same breadth of knowledge, regardless of their perceived or tested ability levels. The Common Core State Standards advocate high academic expectations for all students in English language arts and mathematics. The online "Application to Students with Disabilities" (n.d.) offers facts for students with disabilities, with information on universal design for learning (UDL) as a way for students with disabilities to access the knowledge and skills. As discussed, UDL principles are based on neuroscience and believe that the curriculum should be diversely presented by educators and expressed by students in multiple ways. The universal aspect offers a broad range of goals, methods, materials, and assessments for all students. Preparing teachers how to deliver the curriculum using these principles requires training. As indicated by the sampling of students with disabilities who were honored at the ceremony, no two students are alike, so the learning experiences and coaching experiences also need to differ.

"Students need to show what they know," said Ricki Sabia, a mother of a son with Down syndrome and associate director of the National Down Syndrome Society National Policy Center.

Sabia also talked about RTI connecting with UDL as a way to allow the interventions to work. The Center for Applied Special Technology (CAST, n.d.) offers research-supported classroom strategies. A video from the National Center on Universal Design for Learning (2011) has an overview of how students' unique fingerprints require educators to minimize the barriers and maximize the learning with flexible curriculum that offers more than access, but challenges as well, to fuel each student's interests.

Diversity today seems to be the norm, rather than the exception. The timeless story of Animal School (available on YouTube from 4811jc, 2009) talks about the dangers of stomping out uniqueness. Some disabilities, such as cerebral palsy or Down syndrome, may be visible, while others, such as dyslexia, depression, or traumatic brain injury, may be hidden to the eye, but exist just as well. Students with a spectrum of abilities require a spectrum of teaching approaches, while educators require a spectrum of coaching strategies to duplicate the successes. In addition, society's attitudes often influence accomplishments.

As an educator in the field for several decades, I have heard many disability sentiments from colleagues in the teachers' room, families at parent conferences or individualized education program meetings, and students in kindergarten through graduate-level classrooms about great days and not-so-great days. Ben Yellin, who has a son is in his 20s with an intellectual developmental disability, describes his son as having a 6- to 8-year-old mind in an adult body. He and his wife, as advocates for their son, navigated the school system by thinking outside the parameters to find a way for their son to live independently. The Yellins procured a grant to create a school store at the high school for their son and his classmates to learn functional life skills. "Question everything, shout, and investigate. There is a difference between negligent vs. vigilant and jaded. Think yes!" recommends Yellin.

Many of the students who were honored at the *Yes I Can* ceremony spoke about how when people verbalized what can't be accomplished, the students, along with their support systems of families and educators who believed in them, figured out a way to spin that into "Yes I can!" Their attendance at the ceremony proved just that.

The *Yes I Can* awards offer many lessons that inclusive coaches can duplicate. The strongest one is to share the belief system of how to reach set-upon goals. Collaborative groups within inclusive environments need to first believe that students are capable of high achievements in order for successes to be duplicated.

Source: Designed at Wordle (http://www.wordle.net).

EXAMINING ISSUES AND PERSPECTIVES

Professional learning must be based on research and consistently implemented and supported (Learning Forward, 2011). Inclusion coaching involves many variables, both physical and human. Classroom setups, materials, planning times, supportive staff, students, and families are a few of the variables involved in the laboratory that we call the classroom. The elements of instruction in inclusive, standards-based classrooms involve differentiated instruction and universal design with considerations given to the methods, materials, environment, content, collaboration, and assessment (Voltz, Sims, & Nelson, 2010). The complexities increase since positive perspectives must accompany access. Even though more students are now included in general education classrooms, students with disabilities lag behind their peers in terms of achieving equitable outcomes (Ludlow, 2012).

Inclusion coaching helps all to strategically determine how students with exceptionalities achieve success as they are educated alongside their peers. This includes carefully reviewing student records and levels and responding with instructional approaches that honor the diversity and uniqueness that students present. Intellectual and cultural diversity is embraced and honored with lessons that offer high expectations of learning. Inclusive classrooms provide physical and social environments that examine the issues with welcoming perspectives. Coaches who offer input draw out the best in all staff and students without assuming a hierarchical role, but with a continuum of ongoing and collaborative support.

Figures 15.1 and 15.2 invite inclusion coaches and all collaborative partners to continually implement structured, knowledgeable, compassionate, professional, and reflective practices in their schools and inclusive classrooms.

Figure 15.1 Revisiting Inclusion Rules

Please reflect on how you and your colleagues will continually apply these rules in your inclusive classrooms.

Structure	Awareness	Compassion	Professional Collaboration	Reflection

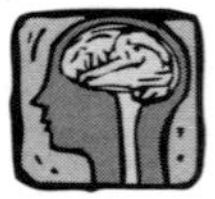

Figure 15.2 Inclusion Coaching Is as Easy as the ABCs

A	ttitudes and awareness
b	egin
c	ompassionate coaching and collaborations.
D	on't
e	ver
f	orget:
G	roups
h	onor
i	nclusion.
J	ust
k	nowing
l	earners'
m	any
n	eeds
o	pens
p	ositive
q	uality
r	eflective relationships that rule!
S	taff are given supports with structure in place.
T	ruly
u	nderstand and
v	alue
w	ork
(e)x	amined
y	early and
z	ealously!

Bibliography

lberta Education. (2009, February). *The principal quality practice guideline: Promoting successful school leadership in Alberta.* Retrieved June 22, 2012, from http://education.alberta.ca/media/949129/principal-quality-practice-guideline-english-12feb09.pdf

Alberta Education. (2009, June). *Setting the direction framework.* Edmonton, AB, Canada: Author.

Algozzine, R., Daunic, A., & Smith, S. (2010). *Preventing problem behaviors: Schoolwide programs and classroom practices.* Thousand Oaks, CA: Corwin.

Allison, S., & Harbour, M. (2009). *The coaching toolkit.* Thousand Oaks, CA: Corwin.

All Things PLC. (n.d.). *Guidelines for applying as a national model of a professional learning community at work.* Retrieved from http://www.allthingsplc.info/evidence/guidelines.php,

Angelle, P., & Bilton, L. (2009). Confronting the unknown: Principal preparation training in issues related to special education. *AASA Journal of Scholarship & Practice, 5*(4), 5–9.

Animoto Productions. (2013). *Unlimited videos for educators.* Retrieved from at http://animoto.com/education

Application to Students with Disabilities. (n.d.). Retrieved from http://www.corestandards.org/assets/application-to-students-with-disabilities.pdf

Armstrong, D., Armstrong, A., & Spandagou, I. (2011). Inclusion: By choice or by chance? *International Journal of Inclusive Education, 15*(1), 29–39.

Austin, V. L. (2001). Teachers' beliefs about co-teaching. *Remedial and Special Education, 22*(4), 245–255.

Banda, D., Grimmett, E., & Hart, S. (2009). Helping students with autism spectrum disorders in general education classrooms manage transition issues. *Teaching Exceptional Children, 41*(4), 16–21.

Bandura, A. (1977). *Social learning theory.* New York: General Learning Press.

Bartalo, D. (2012). *Closing the teaching gap: Coaching for instructional leaders.* Thousand Oaks, CA: Corwin.

Bellanca, R., & Brandt, R. (2010). *21st century skills: Rethinking how students learn.* Bloomington, IN: Solution Tree.

Bellini, S. (2006). *Building social relationships: A systematic approach to teaching social interaction skills to children and adolescents with autism spectrum disorders and other social disorders.* Shawnee Mission, KS: Autism Asperger.

Bernhardt, V. (2002). *The school portfolio toolkit: A planning, implementation, and evaluation guide for continuous school improvement.* Larchmont, NY: Eye on Education.

Billingsley, B. (2007). Recognizing and supporting the critical roles of teachers in special education leadership. *Exceptionality, 15*(3), 163–176.

Binder, J., Zagefka, H., Brown, R., Funke, F., Kessler, T., & Mummendey, A. (2009). Does contact reduce prejudice or does prejudice reduce contact? A longitudinal test of the contact hypothesis among majority and minority groups in three European countries. *Journal of Personality and Social Psychology, 96*, 843–856.

Black, P., & William, D. (1998). Assessment and classroom learning. *Assessment in Education, 5*(1), 7–75.

Bond, R., & Castagnera, E. (2006). Peer supports and inclusive education: An underutilized resource. *Theory Into Practice, 45*(3), 224–229.

Boscardin, M. L. (2005). The administrative role in transforming secondary schools to support inclusive evidence-based practices. *American Secondary Education, 33*(3), 21–32.

Boscardin, M., Mainzer, R., & Kealy, M. (2011). Commentary: A response to "Preparing special education administrators for inclusion in diverse, standards-based contexts," by Deborah L. Voltz and Loucrecia Collins (2010). *Teacher Education and Special Education, 34*(1), 71–78.

Boudah, D. J., Schumacher, J. B., & Deshler, D. D. (1997). Collaborative instruction: Is it an effective option for inclusion in secondary classrooms? *Learning Disability Quarterly, 20*(4), 293–316.

Braden, J. P., Schroder, J. L., & Buckley, J. A. (2001). *Secondary school reform, inclusion, and authentic assessment.* Madison: Wisconsin Center for Education Research.

Brenchley, C. (2012). Launching Project RESPECT. *Homeroom*, February 15. Retrieved from http://www.ed.gov/blog/2012/02/launching-project-respect/

Brooks-Rallins, A. (2011). Tackle challenges and build relationships using tools for meaningful relationships. *JSD, 32*(3), 68–69.

Browder, D., Flowers, C., Ahlgrim-Delzell, L., Karvonen, M., Spooner, F., & Algozzine, R. (2004). The alignment of alternate assessment content with academic and functional curricula. *Journal of Special Education, 37*(4), 211–223.

Brownell, M., Adams, A., Sindelar, P., Waldron, N., & Vanhover, S. (2006). The role of teacher qualities in collaboration. *Exceptional Children, 72*, 169–185.

Bruns, D., & Mogharreban, C. (2007). The gap between beliefs and practices: Early childhood practitioners' perceptions about inclusion. *Journal of Research in Childhood Education, 21*(3), 229.

Bryant, F. (2009). The proper consultant's stance in diversity and inclusion: "Be all you can be" typified by the four "be attitudes." *Diversity Factor, 17*(1), 1–6.

Buell, M. J., Hallam, R., Gamel-McCormick, M., & Sheer, S. (1999). A survey of general and special education teachers' perceptions and in-service needs concerning inclusion. *International Journal of Disability, Development, and Education, 46*(2), 143–156.

Buffum, A., Mattos, M., & Weber, C. (2012). *Simplifying response to intervention: Four essential guiding principles.* Bloomington, IN: Solution Tree.

Bushe, G. R., & Kassam, A. F. (2005). When is appreciative inquiry transformational? A meta-case analysis. *Journal of Applied Behavioral Science, 41*(2), 161–181.

Bybee, R. (2005). *The biological science curriculum study (BSCS).* Retrieved from www.miamisci.org/ph/lpintro5e.html

Campbell, P., Milbourne, S., & Silverman, C. (2001). Strengths-based child portfolios: A professional development activity to alter perspectives of children with special needs. *Topics in Early Childhood Special Education, 21*(3), 152–162.

Carpenter, L., & Dyal, A. (2007). Secondary inclusion: Strategies for implementing the consultative teacher model. *Education, 127*(3), 344–350.

Carter, E., & Kennedy, C. (2006). Promoting access to the general education curriculum using peer support strategies. *Research & Practice for Persons With Severe Disabilities, 31*(4), 284–292.

Carter, E., Moss, C., Hoffman, A., Chung, Y., & Sisco, L. (2011). Efficacy and social validity of peer support arrangements for adolescents with disabilities. *Exceptional Children, 78*(1), 107–125.

Causton-Theoharis, J. N., & Malmgren, K. W. (2005). Increasing peer interaction for students with severe disabilities via paraprofessional training. *Exceptional Children, 71*, 431–444.

Center for Applied Special Technology. (2012). *Transforming education through universal design for learning.* Retrieved from http://www.cast.org/

Center for Applied Special Technology. (n.d.). *About UDL: What is universal design for learning?* Retrieved from http://www.cast.org/udl/

Center for Effective Collaboration and Practice. (n.d.). *Classwide peer tutoring.* Retrieved from http://cecp.air.org/familybriefs/docs/PeerTutoring.pdf

Congdon, M., & Stansbery, S. (2010). Providing immediate feedback to co-teachers through bug-in-ear technology: An effective method of peer coaching in inclusion classrooms. *Teacher Education and Special Education, 33*(1), 83–96.

Cook, B., Shepherd, K., Cook, S., & Cook L. (2012). Facilitating the effective implementation of evidence-based practices through teacher-parent collaboration. *Teaching Exceptional Children, 44*(3), 22–30.

Council of Chief State School Officers & National Governors Association. (2012). *Common Core State Standards Initiative: English language arts standards and mathematics standards.* Retrieved from http://www.corestandards.org/

Council for Exceptional Children. (2013a). *CEC ethical principles and practice standards for special education professionals.* Retrieved from http://www.cec.sped.org/Standards/Ethical-Principles-and-Practice-Standards

Council for Exceptional Children. (2013b). *Professional standards news.* Retrieved from http://www.cec.sped.org/Standards/Standards-for-Professional-Preparation?sc_lang=en

Council for Exceptional Children. (2013c). *Yes I Can! Awards.* Retrieved from http://www.cec.sped.org/About-Us/CEC-Award-Programs/Yes-I-Can-Awards/Yes-I-Can-Award-Winners?sc_lang=en

Crowson, M., & Brandes, J. (2010). Predicting community opposition to inclusion in schools: The role of social dominance, contact, intergroup anxiety, and economic conservatism. *Journal of Psychology, 144*(2), 121–144.

Cullen, J., Gregory, J., Jess, L., & Noto, L. (2010). *The teacher attitudes toward inclusion scale (TAYIS) technical report.* Paper presented at the annual meeting of the Eastern Educational Research Association.

Danielson, C. (2007). *Enhancing professional practice: A framework for teaching* (2nd ed.). Alexandria, VA: ASCD.

Darling-Hammond, L., & Richardson, N. (2009). Teaching learning: What matters? *Educational Leadership, 66*(5), 46–53.

Davis, B. (2008). *How to coach teachers who don't think like you: Using literacy strategies to coach across content areas.* Thousand Oaks, CA: Corwin.

Dewey, J. (1916). Democracy and education. *Infants and Young Children, 16*(4), 296–216.

Disabled World. (2006). *Famous people with disabilities.* Retrieved from http://www.disabled-world.com/artman/publish/article_0060.shtml

Doing What Works. (n.d.). *School principal/reflective leadership strategies.* Retrieved from http://dww.ed.gov/

DuFour, R. (2004). Schools are learning communities. *Educational Leadership, 61*(8), 6–11.

DuFour, R., DuFour, R., & Eaker, R. (2008). *Revisiting professional learning communities at work: New insights for improving schools.* Bloomington, IN: Solution Tree.

DuFour, R., DuFour, R., Eaker, R., & Many, T. (2006). *Learning by doing: A handbook for professional learning communities at work.* Bloomington, IN: Solution Tree.

DuFour, R., & Marzano, R. (2011). *Leaders of learning: How district, school, and classroom leaders improve student achievement.* Bloomington, IN: Solution Tree.

Edwards, C., & Da Fonte, A. (2012). The 5-point plan: Fostering successful partnerships with families of students with disabilities. *Teaching Exceptional Children, 44*(3), 6–13.

Epstein, M., Atkins, M., Cullinan, D., Kutash, K., & Weaver, R. (2008). *Reducing behavior problems in the elementary school classroom: A practice guide* (NCEE #2008–012). Washington, DC: National Center for Education Evaluation and Regional Assistance, Institute of Education Sciences, U.S. Department of Education. Retrieved from http://ies.ed.gov/ncee/wwc/publications/practiceguides

Ervin, R. A. (2008). *Considering tier 3 within a response-to-intervention model.* Retrieved from www.rtinetwork.org

Feinberg, J. (2011). *Wordle.* Retrieved from http://www.wordle.net/

Fialka, J. (2005). Brief, amazing moments of inclusion. *International Journal of Whole Schooling, 1*(2), 15–16.

Fitch, E., & Hulgin, K. (2008). Achieving inclusion through CLAD: Collaborative learning assessment through dialogue. *International Journal of Inclusive Education, 12*(4), 423–439.

4811jc. (2009). *Animal School.* Retrieved from http://www.youtube.com/watch?v=o8limRtHZPs

Fredembach, B., de Boisferon, A. H., & Gentaz, E. (2009). Learning of arbitrary association between visual and auditory novel stimuli in adults: The "bond effect" of haptic exploration. *PLoS ONE, 4*(3), e4844. Retrieved from www.plosone.org

Friend, M., & Cook, L. (2009). *Interactions: Collaboration skills for school professionals* (6th ed.). Boston: Allyn & Bacon.

Gal, E., Schreur, N., & Engel-Yeger, B. (2010). Inclusion of children with disabilities: Teachers' attitudes and requirements for environmental accommodations. *International Journal of Whole Schooling, 25*(2), 89–99.

Galley, M. (2004). Not separate, but equal. *Teacher Magazine, 15*(5), 47.

Gehret, J. (2009). *The don't-give-up kid and learning disabilities* (4th ed.). Fairport, NY: Verbal Images Press.

Gewertz, C. (2007). Soft skills in big demand. In "Ready for what? Preparing students for college careers, and life after high school." *Ed Week,* June 12.

Glazzard, J. (2011). Perceptions of the barriers to effective inclusion in one primary school: Voices of teachers and teaching assistants. *Support for Learning, 26*(2), 56–63.

Goddard, Y. L., Goddard, R. D., & Taschannen-Moran, M. (2007). A theoretical and empirical investigation of teacher collaboration for school improvement and student achievement in public elementary schools. *Teachers College Record, 109*(4), 877–896.

Griffin, C. C., Kilgore, K. L., Winn, J. A., Otis-Willborn, A. (2008). First year special educators' relationships with their general education colleagues. *Teacher Education Quarterly, 35*(1), 141–157.

Guarino, C. M., Santibanez, L., & Daley, G. A. (2006). Teacher recruitment and retention: A review of the recent empirical literature. *Review of Educational Research, 76*(2), 173–208.

Gurgur, H., & Hasan, U. (2010). A phenomenological analysis on the views on co-teaching applications in the inclusion classroom. *Educational Sciences: Theory and Practice, 10*(1), 311–331.

Harrison, C., & Killon, J. (2007). Ten roles for teacher leaders. *Teachers as Leaders, 65*(1), 74–77.

Haskell, D. (2000). Building bridges between science and special education: Inclusion in the science classroom. *Electronic Journal of Science Education, 4*(3). Retrieved from http://wolfweb.unr.edu/homepage/crowther/ejse/haskell.html

Hines, J. (2008). Making collaboration work in inclusive high school classrooms: Recommendations for principals. *Intervention in School & Clinic, 43*(5), 277–28.

Holcomb, E. L. (2012). *Data dynamics: Aligning teacher team, school, & district efforts.* Bloomington, IN: Solution Tree.

InclusionEducation's channel. (n.d.). Retrieved from http://www.youtube.com/user/inclusioneducation

IRIS Center. (n.d.). *Star legacy modules: Accessing the general education curriculum: Inclusion considerations for students with disabilities.* Retrieved from http://iris.peabody.vanderbilt.edu/agc/cresource.htm

Jacobson, D. (2010). Coherent instructional improvement and PLCs: Is it possible to do both? *Phi Delta Kappan, 91*(6), 38–45.

Jenkins, A., & Ornelles, C. (2009). Determining professional development needs of general education educators in teaching students with disabilities in Hawaii. *Professional Development in Education, 35*(4), 635–654.

Jeynes, W. H. (2005). *Parental involvement and student achievement: A meta-analysis. Family Involvement Research Digest.* Cambridge, MA: Harvard Family Research Project. Retrieved from http://www.gse.harvard.edu/hfrp/publications_resources/publications_series/family_involvement_research_digests/parental_involvement_and_student_achievement_a_meta_analysis

Jimenez, B., Browder, D., Spooner, F., & DiBiase, W. (2012). Inclusive inquiry science using peer-mediated embedded instruction for students with moderate intellectual disability. *Exceptional Children, 78*(3), 301–317.

Josephson Institute. (2012). *Character counts.* Retrieved from http://charactercounts.org/sixpillars.html

Kamens, M. W., Loprete, S. J., & Slostad, F. A. (2003). Inclusive classrooms: What practicing teachers want to know. *Action Teacher Education, 25*(1), 20–26.

Kardos, S. M., & Johnson, S. M. (2007). On their own and presumed expert: New teachers' experience with their colleagues. *Teachers College Record, 109*(9), 2083–2106. Retrieved from portal.macam.ac.il/DbImage.aspx?image=file&id=1754

Karten, T. (2007). *More inclusion strategies that work! Aligning student strengths with standards.* Thousand Oaks, CA: Corwin.

Karten, T. (2008a). *Embracing disabilities in the classroom: Strategies to maximize students' assets.* Thousand Oaks, CA: Corwin.

Karten, T. (2008b). *Inclusion activities that work! Grades 6–8.* Thousand Oaks, CA: Corwin.

Karten, T. (2009a). *Inclusion succeeds with effective strategies: Grades K–5* (Laminated guide). Port Chester, NY: National Professional Resources, Dude Publishing.

Karten, T. (2009b). *Inclusion succeeds with effective strategies: Grades 6–12* (Laminated guide). Port Chester, NY: National Professional Resources, Dude Publishing.

Karten, T. (2010a). *Inclusion lesson plan book for 21st century educators.* Port Chester, NY: National Professional Resources.

Karten, T. (2010b). *Inclusion strategies and interventions.* Bloomington, IN: Solution Tree.

Karten, T. (2010c). *Inclusion strategies that work! Research-based methods for the classroom* (2nd ed.). Thousand Oaks, CA: Corwin.

Karten, T. (2011). *Inclusion lesson plan book for the 21st century* (Teacher training edition). Port Chester, NY: Dude Publishing.

Karten, T. (2012a). *Common core standards: Unique practices for inclusive classrooms: English language arts* (Laminated guide). Port Chester, NY: Dude Publishing.

Karten, T. (2012b). *Common core standards: Unique practices for inclusive classrooms: Mathematics* (Laminated guide). Port Chester, NY: National Professional Resources, Dude Publishing.

Katzenmeyer, M., & Moller, G. (2001). *Awakening the sleeping giant: Helping teachers develop as leaders* (2nd ed.). Thousand Oaks, CA: Corwin.

Kee, K., Anderson, K., Dearing, V., Harris, E., & Schuster, F. (2010). *Results coaching: The new essential for school leaders.* Thousand Oaks, CA: Corwin.

Keller, H. (1903). *Optimism: An essay.* New York: T.Y. Crowell.

Kennedy Krieger Institute. (2012). One child with autism: Why a one-size-fits-all approach doesn't work in autism education. *Potential Magazine.* Retrieved from http://www.kennedykrieger.org/potential-online/potential-spring-2009/one-child-autism-why-one-size-fits-all-approach-doesnt-work-autism-education

Khan Academy. (2012). *The one world schoolhouse: Education reimagined.* Retrieved from www.khanacademy.org/

Kids on the Block. (2012). Retrieved from http://www.kotb.com/

Kilanowski-Press, L., Foote, C., & Rinaldo, V. (2010). Inclusion classrooms and teachers: A survey of current practices. *International Journal of Special Education, 25*(3), 43–56.

Killion, J. (2008). *Assessing impact: Evaluating staff development.* Thousand Oaks, CA: Corwin.

Killion, J., & Hirsh, S. (2012). *Meet the promise of content standards: Investing in professional learning.* Oxford, OH: Learning Forward. Retrieved from http://www.learningforward.org/docs/pdf/meetpromiseinvesting.pdf

King-Sears, M. (2008). Facts and fallacies: Differentiation and the general education curriculum for students with special education needs. *Support for Learning, 23*(2), 55–62.

Kingsley, E. P. (1987). *Welcome to Holland.* Retrieved from http://www.our-kids.org/Archives/Holland.html

Knight, J. (2007). *Instructional coaching: A partnership approach to improving instruction.* Thousand Oaks, CA: Corwin.

Knight, J. (Ed.). (2009). *Coaching approaches and perspectives.* Thousand Oaks, CA: Corwin.

Knight, J. (2011). What good coaches do. *Educational Leadership, 69*(2), 18–22.

Knight, J., & Cornett, J. (2008). *Studying the impact of instructional coaching.* University of Kansas: Kansas Coaching Project at the Center for Research on Learning and Department of Special Education. Retrieved from http://instructionalcoach.org/research/tools/paper-studying-the-impact-of-instructional-coaching

Kozik, P., Cooney, B. Vinciguerra, S., Gradel, K., & Black, J. (2009). Promoting inclusion in secondary schools through appreciative inquiry. *American Secondary Education, 38*(1), 77–91.

Kretlow, A., & Blatz, S. (2011). The ABCs of evidence-based practice for teachers. *Teaching Exceptional Children, 43*(5), 8–19.

Learning Forward. (2011). *Standards for professional learning.* Oxford, OH: Author. Retrieved from http://www.learningforward.org/index.cfm

Lee, H. (1960). *To kill a mockingbird.* New York: Grand Central.

Lee, S.-H., Wehmeyer, M., Soukup, J., & Palmer, S. B. (2010). Impact of curriculum modifications on access to the general education curriculum for students with disabilities. *Exceptional Children, 76*(2), 213–233.

Levenson, N. (2011–2012). Academic ROI: What does the most good? *Educational Leadership, 69*(4), 34–39.

Loveless, T. (2012a). *The 2012 Brown Center Report on American Education.* Brookings Institution, February 16. Retrieved from http://www.brookings.edu/research/reports/2012/02/16-brown-education

Loveless, T. (2012b, April 18). Does the common core matter? *Education Week, 31*(28), 32.

Ludlow, B. (2012). Inclusive schools: Moving beyond access to outcomes. *Teaching Exceptional Children, 44*(4), 6.

Maryland State Department of Education. (2012). *School improvement in Maryland: Introduction to the classroom-focused improvement process (CFIP).* Retrieved from http://mdk12.org/process/cfip

Marzo, C. (2010). *Just add water.* Retrieved from http://www.youtube.com/watch?v=Oz5L7RWw8E4

MasteryConnect. (2012). *Time-saving formative assessment tools: Free Common Core app.* Retrieved from http://www.masteryconnect.com/

Mastropieri, M., & Scruggs, T. (2001). How to summarize single-participant research: Ideas and applications. *Exceptionality, 9,* 227–244.

Mastropieri, M., Scruggs, T., & Berkeley, S. (2007). Peers helping peers. *Educational Leadership, 64*(5), 54–58.

McClure, C. (2008). *The benefits of teacher collaboration: Essentials on educational data and research analysis.* Retrieved from http://www.districtadministration.com/article/benefits-teacher-collaboration

McCrimmon, D. (2003). Nothing wrong with being wrong! *Independent School, 62*(3), 12.

Michaelsen, L. K., Bauman Knight, A., & Fink, L. D. (Eds.). (2004). *Team-based learning: A transformative use of small groups in college teaching.* Sterling, VA: Stylus Publishing.

Microsoft. (2013). *AutoSummarize a document in Microsoft Office Word 2007.* Retrieved from http://www.microsoft.com/education/en-us/teachers/how-to/Pages/auto summarize-document.aspx

Moats, L., & Tolman, C. (2008). *Types of reading disability.* Retrieved from www.reading rockets.org/article/28749

Mora, P. (1997). *Tomás and the library lady.* New York: Knopf.

National Association of State Directors of Special Education. (n.d.). *IDEA partnership.* Retrieved from http://www.ideapartnership.org/

National Center on Universal Design for Learning, at CAST. (2011). *Videos about UDL.* Retrieved from http://www.udlcenter.org/resource_library/videos/udlcenter/udl

National Center on Universal Design for Learning, at CAST. (2012). *Videos about UDL.* Retrieved from http://www.udlcenter.org/resource_library/videos/udlcenter/udl

National Council of Teachers of Mathematics. (2012). *Illuminations: Resources for teaching math.* Retrieved from http://illuminations.nctm.org/ActivityDetail.aspx?ID=11

National Dissemination Center for Children with Disabilities. (2010, September). *Transition to adulthood.* Retrieved from http://www.nichcy.org/schoolage/transi tionadult/

National Dissemination Center for Children with Disabilities. (2012, December). *Overview of early intervention.* Retrieved from http://www.nichcy.org/babies/over view/

National Dissemination Center for Children with Disabilities. (n.d.). *Especially for . . . families and communities.* Retrieved from http://nichcy.org/families-community

Neubert, D., & Moon, M. (2006). Postsecondary settings and transition services for students. *Focus on Exceptional Children, 39*(4), 1–8.

Nolet, V., & McLaughlin, M. (2005). *Accessing the general education curriculum. Including students with disabilities in standards-based reform* (2nd ed.). Thousand Oaks, CA: Corwin.

Oluwole, J. (2009). A principal's dilemma: Full inclusion or student's best interests? *Journal of Cases in Educational Leadership, 12*(1), 12–25.

Palincsar, A. S., Magnusson, S. J., Collins, K. M., & Cutter, J. (2001). Making science accessible to all: Results of a design experiment in inclusive classrooms. *Learning Disability Quarterly, 24,* 15–32.

Pany, D., & McCoy, K. M. (1988). Effects of corrective feedback on word accuracy and reading comprehension of readers with learning disabilities. *Journal of Learning Disabilities, 21,* 546–550.

Pashler, H., Bain, P., Bottge, B., Graesser, A., Koedinger, K., McDaniel, M., & Metcalfe, J. (2007). *Organizing instruction and study to improve student learning* (NCER 2007–2004). Washington, DC: National Center for Education Research. Retrieved from http://ncer.ed.gov

Paterson, D. (2007). Teachers' in-flight thinking in inclusive classrooms. *Journal of Learning Disabilities, 40*(5), 427–435.

Pearson Education. (2011). *Assessment Training Institute.* Retrieved from http://www.assessmentinst.com/

Piaget, J. (1926). *Language and thought of the child.* New York: Harcourt, Brace & Company, Inc.

Piaget, J. (1929). *The child's conception of the world.* London: Kegan Paul.

PORTCO. (2010). *Disabilities no obstacle for these 2.* Retrieved from http://portco.org/2010/08/648/

Prizant, B., Wetherby, A., Rubin, E., Laurent, A., & Rydell, P. (2003). *A comprehensive educational approach for children with autism spectrum disorders.* Baltimore: Paul H. Brookes.

Professional Development Partnership. (n.d.). *A common language for professional learning communities.* Retrieved from http://www.state.nj.us/education/profdev/pd/teacher/common.pdf

Project Wisdom. (2013). *Helping students make wiser choices.* Retrieved from http://www.projectwisdom.com/

Raskind, M. H., & Goldberg, R. J. (2005). *Life success for students with learning disabilities: A parent's guide.* Retrieved from http://www.ldonline.org/article/12836/

Ray, D. (2006). *Singing hands.* New York: Clarion.

Reavis, G. (1940s). *Animal school.* Cincinnati, OH: Assistant Superintendent of Schools.

Reeves, D. (2011). *Elements of grading: A guide to effective practice.* Bloomington, IN: Solution Tree.

Rock, D., & Schwartz, J. (2006). The neuroscience of leadership. *Strategy Business.* Retrieved from http://www.strategy-business.com/article/06207?gko=6da0a

Ryan, E. (2012). How to be a visible principal. *ASCD Education Update, 54*(5), 1, 6–7.

Ryan, J., Hughes, E., Katsiyannis, A., McDaniel, M., & Sprinkle, C. (2011). Research-based educational practices for students with autism spectrum disorders. *Teaching Exceptional Children, 43*(3), 56–64.

Salend, S. (2005). *Creating inclusive classrooms: Effective and reflective practices for all students* (5th ed.). Upper Saddle River, NJ: Pearson Education.

Salend, S. (2009). *Classroom testing and assessment for all students: Beyond standardization.* Thousand Oaks, CA: Corwin.

Salend, S. (2012). Teaching students not to sweat the test. *Phi Delta Kappan, 93*(6), 20–25.

Samuels, C. (2011). Finding efficiencies in special education programs. *Education Week, 30*(16), 32–34.

Saunders, W., Goldenberg, C., & Gallimore, R. (2009). Increasing achievement by focusing grade-level teams on improving classroom learning: A prospective, quasi-experimental study of Title I schools. *American Educational Research Journal, 46*(4), 1006–1033.

SCERTS Model. (2012). *Welcome to the SCERTS Model website.* Retrieved from http://www.scerts.com/

Schachter, R. (2012). Seeking saving in special ed. *District Administrator, 48*(1), 36–57.

Scheeler, M. C., Congdon, M., & Stansbery, S. (2011). Providing immediate feedback to co-teachers through bug-in-ear technology: An effective method of peer coaching in inclusion classrooms. *Teacher Education and Special Education, 33*(1), 83–96.

School Administration Publishing. (2012). *School leadership briefing: ISLLC standards.* Retrieved from http://www.schoolbriefing.com/isllc-standards/

Scruggs, T., Mastropieri, M., Berkeley, S., & Graetz, J. (2010). Do special education interventions improve learning of secondary content? A meta-analysis. *Remedial & Special Education, 31*(6), 437–449.

Scruggs, T., Mastropieri, M., & McDuffie, K. (2007). Co-teaching in inclusive classrooms: A metasynthesis of qualitative research. *Exceptional Children, 73*(4), 392–416.

Sileo, Jane M. (2011). Co-teaching: Getting to know your partner. *Teaching Exceptional Children, 43*(5), 32–38.

Solution Tree. (n.d.). *All things PLC.* Retrieved from http://allthingsplc.info/

Sousa, D. (2007). *How the special needs brain learns.* Thousand Oaks, CA: Corwin.

Spence, D. (2007). A roadmap to college and career readiness. *Education Week, 26*(11), 93–96.

Sweeney, D. (2009). *Student centered coaching.* SouthEast Education Network. Retrieved from www.seenmagazine.us/Sections/ArticleDetail/tabid/79/ArticleID/234/smid/403/reftab/292/Default.aspx

Teacher Leadership Exploratory Consortium. (2012). *Teacher Leader Model Standards.* Retrieved from http://www.teacherleaderstandards.org/

ThinkExist.com. (2012a). *Alan Lakein quotes.* Retrieved from http://thinkexist.com/quotation/planning_is_bringing_the_future_into_the_present/194902.html

ThinkExist. (2012b). *Maria Montessori quotes.* Retrieved from http://thinkexist.com/quotation/the_greatest_sign_of_success_for_a_teacher-is_to/215943.html

Tomlinson, C. (1999). *The differentiated classroom: Responding to the needs of all learners.* Alexandria, VA: ASCD.

Tomlinson, C. (2001). *How to differentiate instruction in mixed-ability classrooms* (2nd ed.). Alexandria, VA: ASCD.

Tomlinson, C., & McTighe, J. (2006). *Implementing differentiation of instruction with understanding by design: Connecting content and kids.* Alexandria, VA: ASCD.

Towles-Reeves, E., Kleinert, H., & Muhomba, M. (2009). Alternate assessment: Have we learned anything new? *Exceptional Children, 75*(2), 233–252.

UCtelevision. (2008). *My experience with autism.* Retrieved from http://www.youtube.com/watch?v=2wt1IY3ffoU

U.S. Department of Education. (2003). *Grants: Formula grant definition.* Retrieved from http://www2.ed.gov/fund/grant/about/formgrant.html

U.S. Department of Education. (2010, December 23). *Twenty-ninth annual report to Congress on the implementation of the Individuals with Disabilities Education Act, Parts B and C. 2007.* Retrieved from http://www2.ed.gov/about/reports/annual/osep/2007/parts-b-c/index.html

U.S. Department of Education. (n.d.). *Apply for a grant.* Retrieved from http://www.ed.gov/fund/grants-apply.html

U.S. Department of Education, Institute of Education Sciences. (n.d.). *What works clearinghouse.* Retrieved from http://ies.ed.gov/ncee/wwc/

Villa, R., Thousand, J., & Nevin, A. (2008). *A guide to co-teaching: Practical tips for facilitating student learning.* Thousand Oaks, CA: Corwin.

Villa, R., Thousand, J., & Nevin, A. (2010). *Collaborating with students in instruction and decision-making: The untapped resource.* Thousand Oaks, CA: Corwin.

Voltz, D., Sims, M., & Nelson, B. (2010). *Connecting teachers, students, and standards: Strategies for success in diverse and inclusive classrooms.* Alexandria, VA: ASCD.

Voltz, D., Sims, M., Nelson, B., & Bivens, C. (2008). Engineering successful inclusion in standards-based urban classrooms. *Middle School Journal, 39*(5), 24–30.

Volonino, V., & Zigmond, N. (2007). Promoting research-based practices through inclusion? *Theory Into Practice, 46*(4), 291–300.

Vygotsky, L. (1962). *Thought and language.* Cambridge, MA: MIT Press.

Vygotsky, L. S. (1978). *Mind and society: The development of higher mental processes.* Cambridge, MA: Harvard University Press.

Wang, M., & Brown, R. (2009). Family quality of life: A framework for policy and social service provisions to support families of children with disabilities. *Journal of Family Social Work, 12*(2), 144–167.

Warren, S., Thurlow, M., Christensen, L., Lazarus, S., Moen, R., Davis, K., & Rieke, R. (2011). *Forum on accommodations in the 21st century: Critical considerations for students with disabilities.* Minneapolis: University of Minnesota, National Center on Educational Outcomes, and Washington, DC: Council of Chief State School Officers, Assessing Special Education Students State Collaborative on Assessment and Student Standards.

Wellman, B., & Lipton, L. (2003). *Data-driven dialogue: A facilitator's guide to collaborative inquiry.* Sherman, CT: MiraVia.

Weurlander, M., Soderberg, M., Scheja, M., Hult, H., & Wernerson, A. (2012). Exploring formative assessment as a tool for learning: Students' experiences of different methods of formative assessment. *Assessment & Evaluation in Higher Education, 37*(6), 747–760.

Wiggins, G. (2011). A diploma worth having. *Education Leadership, 66*(6), 28–33.

Wiggins, G., & McTighe, J. (2006). *Understanding by design* (2nd ed.). Upper Saddle River, NJ: Prentice Hall.

William, D. (2011). *Embedded formative assessment.* Bloomington, IN: Solution Tree.

Wiseman, L. (2010). *Multipliers: How the best leaders make everyone smarter.* New York: HarperCollins.

Wolfe, P. (2008). *Brain compatible practices for the classroom: Grades K–6* [DVD]. Port Chester, NY: National Professional Resources.

Wood, J. R. (1992). *The man who loved clowns.* New York: Putnam.

Wright, J. (n.d.). *A curriculum-based measurement: A manual for teachers.* Retrieved from www.jimwrightonline.com/pdfdocs/cbaManual.pdf

Xin, J., & Holmdal, P. (2003). Snacks and skills: Teaching children functional counting skills. *Teaching Exceptional Children, 35*(5), 46–51.

Index

CORWIN

A SAGE Company

The Corwin logo—a raven striding across an open book—represents the union of courage and learning. Corwin is committed to improving education for all learners by publishing books and other professional development resources for those serving the field of PreK–12 education. By providing practical, hands-on materials, Corwin continues to carry out the promise of its motto: **"Helping Educators Do Their Work Better."**